MznLnx

Missing Links Exam Preps

Exam Prep for

Principles of Management

Hill & McShane, 1st Edition

The MznLnx Exam Prep is your link from the texbook and lecture to your exams.
The MznLnx Exam Preps are unauthorized and comprehensive reviews of your textbooks.

All material provided by MznLnx and Rico Publications (c) 2010
Textbook publishers and textbook authors do not particpate in or contribute to these reviews.

MznLnx

Rico
Publications

Exam Prep for Principles of Management
1st Edition
Hill & McShane

Publisher: Raymond Houge
Assistant Editor: Michael Rouger
Text and Cover Designer: Lisa Buckner
Marketing Manager: Sara Swagger
Project Manager, Editorial Production: Jerry Emerson
Art Director: Vernon Lowerui

Product Manager: Dave Mason
Editorial Assitant: Rachel Guzmanji
Pedagogy: Debra Long
Cover Image: Jim Reed/Getty Images
Text and Cover Printer: City Printing, Inc.
Compositor: Media Mix, Inc.

(c) 2010 Rico Publications
ALL RIGHTS RESERVED. No part of this work covered by the copyright may be reproduced or used in any form or by an means--graphic, electronic, or mechanical, including photocopying, recording, taping, Web distribution, information storage, and retrieval systems, or in any other manner--without the written permission of the publisher.

Printed in the United States
ISBN:

For more information about our products, contact us at:
Dave.Mason@RicoPublications.com

For permission to use material from this text or product, submit a request online to:
Dave.Mason@RicoPublications.com

Contents

CHAPTER 1
Management — 1

CHAPTER 2
The External and Internal Environments — 6

CHAPTER 3
Globalization and the Manager — 15

CHAPTER 4
Stakeholders, Ethics, and Corporate Social Responsibility — 23

CHAPTER 5
Planning and Decision Making — 26

CHAPTER 6
Strategy — 32

CHAPTER 7
Managing Operations — 39

CHAPTER 8
Organizing — 47

CHAPTER 9
Control Systems — 50

CHAPTER 10
Organizational Culture — 52

CHAPTER 11
Developing High-Performance Teams — 55

CHAPTER 12
Staffing and Developing a Diverse Workforce — 58

CHAPTER 13
Motivating and Rewarding Employee Performance — 68

CHAPTER 14
Managing Employee Attitudes and Well-Being — 76

CHAPTER 15
Managing through Power, Influence, and Negotiation — 80

CHAPTER 16
Effective Leadership — 83

CHAPTER 17
Communication — 86

CHAPTER 18
Managing Innovation and Change — 88

ANSWER KEY — 95

TO THE STUDENT

COMPREHENSIVE

The *MznLnx* Exam Prep series is designed to help you pass your exams. Editors at MznLnx review your textbooks and then prepare these practice exams to help you master the textbook material. Unlike study guides, workbooks, and practice tests provided by the texbook publisher and textbook authors, *MznLnx* gives you **all** of the material in each chapter in exam form, not just samples, so you can be sure to nail your exam.

MECHANICAL

The MznLnx Exam Prep series creates exams that will help you learn the subject matter as well as test you on your understanding. Each question is designed to help you master the concept. Just working through the exams, you gain an understanding of the subject--its a simple mechanical process that produces success.

INTEGRATED STUDY GUIDE AND REVIEW

MznLnx is not just a set of exams designed to test you, its also a comprehensive review of the subject content. Each exam question is also a review of the concept, making sure that you will get the answer correct without having to go to other sources of material. You learn as you go! Its the easiest way to pass an exam.

HUMOR

Studying can be tedious and dry. MznLnx's instructional design includes moderate humor within the exam questions on occassion, to break the tedium and revitalize the brain

Chapter 1. Management

1. A _____ is a list of the general tasks and responsibilities of a position. Typically, it also includes to whom the position reports, specifications such as the qualifications needed by the person in the job, salary range for the position, etc. A _____ is usually developed by conducting a job analysis, which includes examining the tasks and sequences of tasks necessary to perform the job.
   a. Recruitment
   b. Recruitment Process Insourcing
   c. Recruitment advertising
   d. Job description

2. _____ refers to the stock of skills and knowledge embodied in the ability to perform labor so as to produce economic value. It is the skills and knowledge gained by a worker through education and experience. Many early economic theories refer to it simply as labor, one of three factors of production, and consider it to be a fungible resource -- homogeneous and easily interchangeable.
   a. Deflation
   b. Human capital
   c. Market structure
   d. Productivity management

3. In economics and sociology, an _____ is any factor (financial or non-financial) that enables or motivates a particular course of action, or counts as a reason for preferring one choice to the alternatives. It is an expectation that encourages people to behave in a certain way. Since human beings are purposeful creatures, the study of _____ structures is central to the study of all economic activity (both in terms of individual decision-making and in terms of co-operation and competition within a larger institutional structure.)
   a. A4e
   b. AAAI
   c. A Stake in the Outcome
   d. Incentive

4. _____ for short is a descriptive term for certain executives in a business operation. It is also a formal title held by some business executives, most commonly in the hospitality industry.

   A _____ has broad, overall responsibility for a business or organization. Whereas a manager may be responsible for one functional area, the _____ is responsible for all areas.

   a. Managing director
   b. Chief knowledge officer
   c. Chief technology officer
   d. General manager

5. A _____ or chief executive is one of the highest-ranking corporate officer (executive) or administrator in charge of total management. An individual selected as President and _____ of a corporation, company, organization, or agency, reports to the board of directors. In internal communication and press releases, many companies capitalize the term and those of other high positions, even when they are not proper nouns.
   a. Chief brand officer
   b. Chief executive officer
   c. Financial analyst
   d. Purchasing manager

6. While _____ literally refers to a person responsible for the performance of duties involved in running an organization, the exact meaning of the role is variable, depending on the organization.

While there is no clear line between executive or principal and inferior officers, principal officers are high-level officials in the executive branch of U.S. government such as department heads of independent agencies. In Humphrey's Executor v. United States, 295 U.S. 602 (1935), the Court distinguished between _____s and quasi-legislative or quasi-judicial officers by stating that the former serve at the pleasure of the President and may be removed at his discretion.

   a. Easement
   b. Unreported employment
   c. Australian Fair Pay and Conditions Standard
   d. Executive officer

7. The _____ of a company or public agency is the corporate officer primarily responsible for managing the financial risks of the business or agency. This officer is also responsible for financial planning and record-keeping, as well as financial reporting to higher management. (In recent years, however, the role has expanded to encompass communicating financial performance and forecasts to the analyst community.)
   a. 28-hour day
   b. 1990 Clean Air Act
   c. Chief financial officer
   d. 33 Strategies of War

8. A _____ or chief operations officer is a corporate officer responsible for managing the day-to-day activities of the corporation and for operations management (OM.) The _____ is one of the highest-ranking members of an organization's senior management, monitoring the daily operations of the company and reporting to the board of directors and the top executive officer, usually the chief executive officer (CEO.) The _____ is usually an executive or senior officer.

a. Product innovation
b. Chief operating officer
c. Value based pricing
d. Supervisory board

9. A _____ is an executive position whose holder is focused on scientific and technical issues within an organization. Essentially, a _____ is responsible for the transformation of capital - be it monetary, intellectual, or political - into technology in furtherance of the company's objectives.

The title is most typically found in organizations which significantly develop or exploit information technology.

a. Chief knowledge officer
b. Chief technology officer
c. General Manager
d. Managing director

10. In politics, a _____, (by metaphor with the carved _____ at the prow of a sailing ship), is a person who holds an important title or office yet executes little actual power, most commonly limited by convention rather than law. Common _____s include constitutional monarchs, such as: Queen Elizabeth II, the Emperor of Japan, or presidents in parliamentary democracies, such as the President of Israel.

While the authority of a _____ is in practice generally symbolic, public opinion, respect for the office or the office holder and access to high levels of government can give them significant influence on events.

a. Figurehead
b. 28-hour day
c. 1990 Clean Air Act
d. 33 Strategies of War

11. _____ has been described as the 'process of social influence in which one person can enlist the aid and support of others in the accomplishment of a common task' . A definition more inclusive of followers comes from Alan Keith of Genentech who said '_____ is ultimately about creating a way for people to contribute to making something extraordinary happen.'

_____ is one of the most salient aspects of the organizational context. However, defining _____ has been challenging.

a. Leadership
b. 1990 Clean Air Act
c. Situational leadership
d. 28-hour day

12. An _____ is a person who has possession of an enterprise and assumes significant accountability for the inherent risks and the outcome. It is an ambitious leader who combines land, labor, and capital to create and market new goods or services. The term is a loanword from French and was first defined by the Irish economist Richard Cantillon.
   a. A4e
   b. Entrepreneur
   c. AAAI
   d. A Stake in the Outcome

13. There are two types of _____ relationships: formal and informal. Informal relationships develop on their own between partners. Formal _____, on the other hand, refers to assigned relationships, often associated with organizational _____ programs designed to promote employee development or to assist at-risk children and youth.
   a. Human resource management system
   b. Fix it twice
   c. Real Property Administrator
   d. Mentoring

14. The _____ is a term that was popularised by David McClelland and describes a person's need to feel a sense of involvement and 'belonging' within a social group. However, it should be recognised that McClellend's thinking was strongly influenced by the pioneering work of Henry Murray who first identified underlying psychological human needs and motivational processes (1938.) It was Murray who set out a taxonomy of needs, including Achievement, Power and Affiliation - and placed these in the context of an integrated motivational model.
   a. Need for affiliation
   b. Strong-Campbell Interest Inventory
   c. SESAMO
   d. Polynomial conjoint measurement

15. In law, _____ is the term to describe a partnership between two or more parties.

Chapter 1. Management

In England a number of statutes on the subject have been passed, the chief being the Bastardy Act of 1845, and the Bastardy Laws Amendment Acts of 1872 and 1873. The mother of a bastard may summon the putative father to petty sessions within twelve months of the birth (or at any later time if he is proved to have contributed to the child's support within twelve months after the birth), and the justices, as after hearing evidence on both sides, may, if the mother's evidence be corroborated in some material particular, adjudge the man to be the putative father of the child, and order him to pay a sum not exceeding five shillings a week for its maintenance, together with a sum for expenses incidental to the birth, or the funeral expenses, if it has died before the date of order, and the costs of the proceedings.

a. Affiliation
b. Abraham Harold Maslow
c. Adam Smith
d. Affiliation

Chapter 2. The External and Internal Environments

1. _____ refers to the stock of skills and knowledge embodied in the ability to perform labor so as to produce economic value. It is the skills and knowledge gained by a worker through education and experience. Many early economic theories refer to it simply as labor, one of three factors of production, and consider it to be a fungible resource -- homogeneous and easily interchangeable.
    a. Market structure
    b. Productivity management
    c. Deflation
    d. Human capital

2. _____ is a strategic planning method used to evaluate the Strengths, Weaknesses, Opportunities, and Threats involved in a project or in a business venture. It involves specifying the objective of the business venture or project and identifying the internal and external factors that are favorable and unfavorable to achieving that objective. The technique is credited to Albert Humphrey, who led a convention at Stanford University in the 1960s and 1970s using data from Fortune 500 companies.
    a. SWOT analysis
    b. Marketing
    c. Corporate image
    d. Market share

3. A _____ is a process in which a potential employee is evaluated by an employer for prospective employment in their company, organization and was established in the late 16th century.

A _____ typically precedes the hiring decision, and is used to evaluate the candidate. The interview is usually preceded by the evaluation of submitted résumés from interested candidates, then selecting a small number of candidates for interviews.

   a. Payrolling
   b. Supported employment
   c. Split shift
   d. Job interview

4. A _____ is a name or trademark connected with a product or producer. _____s have become increasingly important components of culture and the economy, now being described as 'cultural accessories and personal philosophies'.

Some people distinguish the psychological aspect of a _____ from the experiential aspect.

a. Brand extension
b. Brand awareness
c. Brand loyalty
d. Brand

5. _____, in marketing, consists of a consumer's commitment to repurchase or otherwise continue using the brand and can be demonstrated by repeated buying of a product or service or other positive behaviors such as word of mouth advocacy.

_____ is more than simple repurchasing, however. Customers may repurchase a brand due to situational constraints, a lack of viable alternatives, or out of convenience.

a. Brand loyalty
b. Brand extension
c. Brand image
d. Brand awareness

6. _____, in microeconomics, are the cost advantages that a business obtains due to expansion. They are factors that cause a producer's average cost per unit to fall as scale is increased. _____ is a long run concept and refers to reductions in unit cost as the size of a facility, or scale, increases.
a. Economies of scope
b. A4e
c. A Stake in the Outcome
d. Economies of scale

7. _____ is a concept related to the relative abilities of parties in a situation to exert influence over each other. If both parties are on an equal footing in a debate, then they will have equal _____, such as in a perfectly competitive market, or between an evenly matched monopoly and monopsony.

There are a number of fields where the concept of _____ has proven crucial to coherent analysis: game theory, labour economics, collective bargaining arrangements, diplomatic negotiations, settlement of litigation, the price of insurance, and any negotiation in general.

a. Trade credit
b. 1990 Clean Air Act
c. Buy-sell agreement
d. Bargaining power

8. In economics, business, retail, and accounting, a _____ is the value of money that has been used up to produce something, and hence is not available for use anymore. In economics, a _____ is an alternative that is given up as a result of a decision. In business, the _____ may be one of acquisition, in which case the amount of money expended to acquire it is counted as _____.
   a. Cost
   b. Cost allocation
   c. Fixed costs
   d. Cost overrun

9. Switching barriers or _____s are terms used in microeconomics, strategic management, and marketing to describe any impediment to a customer's changing of suppliers.

In many markets, consumers are forced to incur costs when switching from one supplier to another. These costs are called _____s and can come in many different shapes.

   a. Strategic business unit
   b. Corporate strategy
   c. Switching cost
   d. Strategic group

10. A _____ is something for which there is demand, but which is supplied without qualitative differentiation across a market. It is a product that is the same no matter who produces it, such as petroleum, notebook paper, or milk. In other words, copper is copper.
   a. 1990 Clean Air Act
   b. 33 Strategies of War
   c. 28-hour day
   d. Commodity

11. In economics, _____ is the desire to own something and the ability to pay for it. The term _____ signifies the ability or the willingness to buy a particular commodity at a given point of time.
   a. 33 Strategies of War
   b. 28-hour day
   c. 1990 Clean Air Act
   d. Demand

12. _____ is an increasingly broadening term with which an organization, or other human system describes the combination of traditionally administrative personnel functions with acquisition and application of skills, knowledge and experience, Employee Relations and resource planning at various levels. The field draws upon concepts developed in Industrial/Organizational Psychology and System Theory. _____ has at least two related interpretations depending on context. The original usage derives from political economy and economics, where it was traditionally called labor, one of four factors of production although this perspective is changing as a function of new and ongoing research into more strategic approaches at national levels. This first usage is used more in terms of '_____ development', and can go beyond just organizations to the level of nations . The more traditional usage within corporations and businesses refers to the individuals within a firm or agency, and to the portion of the organization that deals with hiring, firing, training, and other personnel issues, typically referred to as `_____ management'.

a. Progressive discipline
b. Bradford Factor
c. Human resource management
d. Human resources

13. _____ is a concept in economics which refers to the extent to which an enterprise or a nation actually uses its installed productive capacity. Thus, it refers to the relationship between actual output that 'is' produced with the installed equipment and the potential output which 'could' be produced with it, if capacity was fully used.

If market demand grows, _____ will rise.

a. Diseconomies of scale
b. Factors of production
c. Capacity utilization
d. Multifactor productivity

14. In economics, _____ are obstacles in the path of a firm which wants to leave a given market or industrial sector. These obstacles often cost the firm financially to leave the market and may prohibit it doing so.

If the barriers of exit are significant; a firm may be forced to continue competing in a market, as the costs of leaving may be higher than those incurred if they continue competing in the market.

a. 28-hour day
b. 33 Strategies of War
c. 1990 Clean Air Act
d. Barriers to exit

15. In economics, _____ are business expenses that are not dependent on the activities of the business They tend to be time-related, such as salaries or rents being paid per month. This is in contrast to variable costs, which are volume-related (and are paid per quantity.)

In management accounting, _____ are defined as expenses that do not change in proportion to the activity of a business, within the relevant period or scale of production.

a. Cost of quality
b. Transaction cost
c. Cost allocation
d. Fixed costs

16. _____ is a dynamic of being mutually and physically responsible to and sharing a common set of principles with others. This concept differs distinctly from 'dependence' in that an interdependent relationship implies that all participants are emotionally, economically, ecologically and or morally 'interdependent.' Some people advocate freedom or independence as a sort of ultimate good; others do the same with devotion to one's family, community, or society. _____ recognizes the truth in each position and weaves them together.

a. A4e
b. Interdependence
c. A Stake in the Outcome
d. AAAI

17. _____ is a term used to describe businesses that directly sell a product (or products) or service (or services) that complement the product or service of another company by adding value to mutual customers; for example, Intel and Microsoft (Pentium processors and Windows), or Microsoft ' McAfee (Microsoft Windows ' McAfee anti-virus.)

_____ are sometimes called 'The Sixth Force' (from Porter's Five Forces model), a term which was coined by Adam Brandenburger.

Before its use in business, the word was used to describe a color that is complementory to another color.

a. Strategic group
b. Strategic thinking
c. Strategic drift
d. Complementors

18. _____ is the increase in the amount of the goods and services produced by an economy over time and is dependent on an increase in the creation of money. Growth is conventionally measured as the percent rate of increase in real gross domestic product, or real GDP. GDP is usually calculated in real terms, i.e. inflation-adjusted terms, in order to net out the effect of inflation on the price of the goods and services produced.

a. Economic growth
b. AAAI
c. A4e
d. A Stake in the Outcome

19. _____ or _____ data refers to selected population characteristics as used in government, marketing or opinion research, or the _____ profiles used in such research. Note the distinction from the term 'demography' Commonly-used _____s include race, age, income, disabilities, mobility (in terms of travel time to work or number of vehicles available), educational attainment, home ownership, employment status, and even location.
a. Adam Smith
b. Abraham Harold Maslow
c. Demographic
d. Affiliation

20. In finance, the _____s between two currencies specifies how much one currency is worth in terms of the other. It is the value of a foreign nation's currency in terms of the home nation's currency. For example an _____ of 102 Japanese yen to the United States dollar means that JPY 102 is worth the same as USD 1.
a. A Stake in the Outcome
b. A4e
c. AAAI
d. Exchange rate

21. In economics, _____ is a rise in the general level of prices of goods and services in an economy over a period of time. When the general price level rises, each unit of the functional currency buys fewer goods and services; consequently, _____ is a decline in the real value of money--a loss of purchasing power in the internal medium of exchange which is also the monetary unit of account in an economy. A chief measure of general price-level _____ is the general _____ rate, which is the percentage change in a general price index (normally the Consumer Price Index) over time.
a. A4e
b. Economy
c. A Stake in the Outcome
d. Inflation

22. _____ in its literal sense is the process of transformation of local or regional phenomena into global ones. It can be described as a process by which the people of the world are unified into a single society and function together.

This process is a combination of economic, technological, sociocultural and political forces.

a. Globalization
b. Histogram
c. Cost Management
d. Collaborative Planning, Forecasting and Replenishment

23. A broad definition of _____ is the action of gathering, analyzing, and distributing information about products, customers, competitors and any aspect of the environment needed to support executives and managers in making strategic decisions for an organization.

Key points of this definitions:

1. _____ is an ethical and legal business practice. (This is important as _____ professionals emphasize that the discipline is not the same as industrial espionage which is both unethical and usually illegal.)
2. The focus is on the external business environment.
3. There is a process involved in gathering information, converting it into intelligence and then utilizing this in business decision making. _____ professionals emphasize that if the intelligence gathered is not usable (or actionable) then it is not intelligence.

A more focused definition of _____ regards it as the organizational function responsible for the early identification of risks and opportunities in the market before they become obvious. Experts also call this process the early signal analysis. This definition focuses attention on the difference between dissemination of widely available factual information (such as market statistics, financial reports, newspaper clippings) performed by functions such as libraries and information centers, and _____ which is a perspective on developments and events aimed at yielding a competitive edge.

a. Competitor or Competitive Intelligence
b. 28-hour day
c. 1990 Clean Air Act
d. Competitive intelligence

24. _____ is a theory in evolutionary biology which states that most sexually reproducing species will experience little evolutionary change for most of their geological history (in an extended state called stasis.) When evolution occurs, it is localized in rare, rapid events of branching speciation (called cladogenesis.) Cladogenesis is simply the process by which species split into two distinct species, rather than one species gradually transforming into another.
a. 33 Strategies of War
b. 28-hour day
c. 1990 Clean Air Act
d. Punctuated equilibrium

Chapter 2. The External and Internal Environments

25. _____ is one of the managerial functions like planning, organizing, staffing and directing. It is an important function because it helps to check the errors and to take the corrective action so that deviation from standards are minimized and stated goals of the organization are achieved in desired manner. According to modern concepts, _____ is a foreseeing action whereas earlier concept of _____ was used only when errors were detected. _____ in management means setting standards, measuring actual performance and taking corrective action.
   a. Decision tree pruning
   b. Turnover
   c. Schedule of reinforcement
   d. Control

26. The goal of _____ is to create an organization which will be able to continuously create value for present and future customers, optimizing and organizing it self. Some under _____ understand building blocks which are mandatory for the growth of the organization. To design an organization means to set up a stage where the drama of life will take place.
   a. A4e
   b. AAAI
   c. Organizational architecture
   d. A Stake in the Outcome

27. _____ is an idea in the field of Organizational studies and management which describes the psychology, attitudes, experiences, beliefs and Values (personal and cultural values) of an organization. It has been defined as 'the specific collection of values and norms that are shared by people and groups in an organization and that control the way they interact with each other and with stakeholders outside the organization.'

This definition continues to explain organizational values also known as 'beliefs and ideas about what kinds of goals members of an organization should pursue and ideas about the appropriate kinds or standards of behavior organizational members should use to achieve these goals. From organizational values develop organizational norms, guidelines or expectations that prescribe appropriate kinds of behavior by employees in particular situations and control the behavior of organizational members towards one another.'

_____ is not the same as corporate culture.

   a. Organizational culture
   b. Organizational development
   c. Organizational effectiveness
   d. Union shop

28. The _____ is an economic tool used to determine the strategic resources available to a firm. The fundamental principle of the _____ is that the basis for a competitive advantage of a firm lies primarily in the application of the bundle of valuable resources at the firm's disposal (Wernerfelt, 1984, p172; Rumelt, 1984, p557-558.) To transform a short-run competitive advantage into a sustained competitive advantage requires that these resources are heterogeneous in nature and not perfectly mobile (Barney, 1991, p105-106; Peteraf, 1993, p180).

  a. Resource-based view
  b. Business philosophy
  c. Catfish effect
  d. Frenemy

Chapter 3. Globalization and the Manager

1. _____ in its literal sense is the process of transformation of local or regional phenomena into global ones. It can be described as a process by which the people of the world are unified into a single society and function together.

This process is a combination of economic, technological, sociocultural and political forces.

   a. Histogram
   b. Globalization
   c. Collaborative Planning, Forecasting and Replenishment
   d. Cost Management

2. _____ is subcontracting a process, such as product design or manufacturing, to a third-party company. The decision to outsource is often made in the interest of lowering cost or making better use of time and energy costs, redirecting or conserving energy directed at the competencies of a particular business, or to make more efficient use of land, labor, capital, (information) technology and resources. _____ became part of the business lexicon during the 1980s.
   a. Unemployment insurance
   b. Opinion leadership
   c. Operant conditioning
   d. Outsourcing

3. A market economy is an economy based on the division of labor in which the prices of goods and services are determined in a free price system set by supply and demand. This is often contrasted with a planned economy, in which a central government determines the price of goods and services using a fixed price system. _____ are contrasted with mixed economy where the price system is not entirely free but under some government control that is not extensive enough to constitute a planned economy.
   a. Knowledge Revolution
   b. 1990 Clean Air Act
   c. 28-hour day
   d. Market economies

4. _____ is the political philosophy and practice derived from the works of Karl Marx and Friedrich Engels, though the name '_____' has been used by many with political perspectives those men would likely reject. _____ is a political-economic theory that presents a materialist conception of history, a non-capitalist vision of capitalism and other types of society, and a non-religious view of human liberation. Closely related to the ideology of communism.
   a. Adam Smith
   b. Abraham Harold Maslow
   c. Karl Heinrich Marx
   d. Marxism

5. In economics, business, retail, and accounting, a _____ is the value of money that has been used up to produce something, and hence is not available for use anymore. In economics, a _____ is an alternative that is given up as a result of a decision. In business, the _____ may be one of acquisition, in which case the amount of money expended to acquire it is counted as _____.

a. Fixed costs
b. Cost allocation
c. Cost overrun
d. Cost

6. _____ in its classic form is defined as a company from one country making a physical investment into building a factory in another country. It is the establishment of an enterprise by a foreigner. Its definition can be extended to include investments made to acquire lasting interest in enterprises operating outside of the economy of the investor.

a. Headquarters
b. Compensation methods
c. Business Roundtable
d. Foreign direct investment

7. _____ is a type of trade policy that allows traders to act and transact without interference from government. Thus, the policy permits trading partners mutual gains from trade, with goods and services produced according to the theory of comparative advantage.

Under a _____ policy, prices are a reflection of true supply and demand, and are the sole determinant of resource allocation.

a. 1990 Clean Air Act
b. Free Trade
c. 33 Strategies of War
d. 28-hour day

8. _____ is a designated group of countries that have agreed to eliminate tariffs, quotas and preferences on most (if not all) goods and services traded between them. It can be considered the second stage of economic integration. Countries choose this kind of economic integration form if their economical structures are complementary.

a. Free trade area
b. 1990 Clean Air Act
c. 33 Strategies of War
d. 28-hour day

Chapter 3. Globalization and the Manager

9. The _____ was the outcome of the failure of negotiating governments to create the International Trade Organization (ITO.) GATT was formed in 1947 and lasted until 1994, when it was replaced by the World Trade Organization. The Bretton Woods Conference had introduced the idea for an organization to regulate trade as part of a larger plan for economic recovery after World War II.
   a. 1990 Clean Air Act
   b. Multilateral treaty
   c. 28-hour day
   d. General Agreement on Tariffs and Trade

10. _____ is exchange of capital, goods, and services across international borders or territories. In most countries, it represents a significant share of gross domestic product (GDP.) While _____ has been present throughout much of history, its economic, social, and political importance has been on the rise in recent centuries.
    a. A4e
    b. AAAI
    c. A Stake in the Outcome
    d. International trade

11. The _____ is a trilateral trade bloc in North America created by the governments of the United States, Canada, and Mexico. The agreement creating the trade bloc came into force on January 1, 1994. It superseded the Canada-United States Free Trade Agreement between the U.S. and Canada.
    a. Business war game
    b. Trade union
    c. Career portfolios
    d. North American Free Trade Agreement

12. A _____ is a general term that describes any government policy or regulation that restricts international trade. The barriers can take many forms, including the following terms that include many restrictions in international trade within multiple countries that import and export any items of trade.

    - Import duty
    - Import licenses
    - Export licenses
    - Import quotas
    - Tariffs
    - Subsidies
    - Non-tariff barriers to trade
    - Voluntary Export Restraints
    - Local Content Requirements
    - Embargo

Chapter 3. Globalization and the Manager

Most _____s work on the same principle: the imposition of some sort of cost on trade that raises the price of the traded products. If two or more nations repeatedly use _____s against each other, then a trade war results.

a. Trade creation
b. Customs brokerage
c. Most favoured nation
d. Trade barrier

13. _____ is a system of intermodal freight transport using standard intermodal containers that are standardised by the International Organization for Standardization (ISO.) These can be loaded and sealed intact onto container ships, railroad cars, planes, and trucks.
a. 33 Strategies of War
b. Containerization
c. 1990 Clean Air Act
d. 28-hour day

14. A _____ is someone who helps a group of people understand their common objectives and assists them to plan to achieve them without taking a particular position in the discussion. The _____ will try to assist the group in achieving a consensus on any disagreements that preexist or emerge in the meeting so that it has a strong basis for future action. The role has been likened to that of a midwife who assists in the process of birth but is not the producer of the end result.
a. 33 Strategies of War
b. 1990 Clean Air Act
c. Facilitator
d. 28-hour day

15. _____ is a broad label that refers to any individuals or households that use goods and services generated within the economy. The concept of a _____ is used in different contexts, so that the usage and significance of the term may vary.

Typically when business people and economists talk of _____s they are talking about person as _____, an aggregated commodity item with little individuality other than that expressed in the buy/not-buy decision.

Chapter 3. Globalization and the Manager

   a. 28-hour day
   b. 33 Strategies of War
   c. Consumer
   d. 1990 Clean Air Act

16. A _____ or transnational corporation is a corporation or enterprise that manages production or delivers services in more than one country. It can also be referred to as an international corporation.

The first modern _____ is generally thought to be the Dutch East India Company, established in 1602.

   a. Command center
   b. Small and medium enterprises
   c. Financial Accounting Standards Board
   d. Multinational corporation

17. _____, in microeconomics, are the cost advantages that a business obtains due to expansion. They are factors that cause a producer's average cost per unit to fall as scale is increased. _____ is a long run concept and refers to reductions in unit cost as the size of a facility, or scale, increases.
   a. Economies of scope
   b. A Stake in the Outcome
   c. Economies of scale
   d. A4e

18. Network externalities resemble economies of scale, but they are not considered such because they are a function of the number of users of a good or service in an industry, not of the production efficiency within a business. _____ are only considered examples of network externalities if they are driven by demand side economies.

Formally, a production function > is defined to have:

- constant returns to scale if (for any constant a greater than or equal to 0) >
- increasing returns to scale if (for any constant a greater than 1) >
- decreasing returns to scale if (for any constant a greater than 1) >

where K and L are factors of production, capital and labour, respectively.

Chapter 3. Globalization and the Manager

As an example, the Cobb-Douglas functional form has constant returns to scale when the sum of the exponents adds up to one.

a. A4e
b. AAAI
c. A Stake in the Outcome
d. Economies of scale external to the firm

19. _____ refers to the methods of practicing and using another person's business philosophy. The franchisor grants the independent operator the right to distribute its products, techniques, and trademarks for a percentage of gross monthly sales and a royalty fee. Various tangibles and intangibles such as national or international advertising, training, and other support services are commonly made available by the franchisor.

a. 1990 Clean Air Act
b. ServiceMaster
c. Franchising
d. 28-hour day

20. A _____ is an entity formed between two or more parties to undertake economic activity together. The parties agree to create a new entity by both contributing equity, and they then share in the revenues, expenses, and control of the enterprise. The venture can be for one specific project only, or a continuing business relationship such as the Fuji Xerox _____.

a. Meritor Savings Bank v. Vinson
b. Patent
c. Joint venture
d. Civil Rights Act of 1991

21. A _____, in business matters, is an entity that is controlled by a bigger and more powerful entity. The controlled entity is called a company, corporation, or limited liability company and in some cases can be a government or state-owned enterprise, and the controlling entity is called its parent (or the parent company.) The reason for this distinction is that a lone company cannot be a _____ of any organization; only an entity representing a legal fiction as a separate entity can be a _____.

a. 28-hour day
b. 1990 Clean Air Act
c. 33 Strategies of War
d. Subsidiary

Chapter 3. Globalization and the Manager

22. An _____ is a person who has possession of an enterprise and assumes significant accountability for the inherent risks and the outcome. It is an ambitious leader who combines land, labor, and capital to create and market new goods or services. The term is a loanword from French and was first defined by the Irish economist Richard Cantillon.

    a. A Stake in the Outcome
    b. A4e
    c. AAAI
    d. Entrepreneur

23. An _____ is a person temporarily or permanently residing in a country and culture other than that of the person's upbringing or legal residence. The word comes from the Latin ex and patria (country, fatherland.)

    The term is sometimes used in the context of Westerners living in non-Western countries, although it is also used to describe Westerners living in other Western countries, such as Americans living in the United Kingdom, or Britons living in Spain.

    a. AAAI
    b. A4e
    c. A Stake in the Outcome
    d. Expatriate

24. A _____ is a process in which a potential employee is evaluated by an employer for prospective employment in their company, organization and was established in the late 16th century.

    A _____ typically precedes the hiring decision, and is used to evaluate the candidate. The interview is usually preceded by the evaluation of submitted résumés from interested candidates, then selecting a small number of candidates for interviews.

    a. Split shift
    b. Payrolling
    c. Supported employment
    d. Job interview

25. The _____ captures an expanded spectrum of values and criteria for measuring organizational success: economic, ecological and social. With the ratification of the United Nations and ICLEI _____ standard for urban and community accounting in early 2007, this became the dominant approach to public sector full cost accounting. Similar UN standards apply to natural capital and human capital measurement to assist in measurements required by _____, e.g. the ecoBudget standard for reporting ecological footprint.

a. 1990 Clean Air Act
b. 33 Strategies of War
c. 28-hour day
d. Triple bottom line

Chapter 4. Stakeholders, Ethics, and Corporate Social Responsibility

1. _____ is a form of applied ethics that examines ethical principles and moral or ethical problems that arise in a business environment. It applies to all aspects of business conduct and is relevant to the conduct of individuals and business organizations as a whole. Applied ethics is a field of ethics that deals with ethical questions in many fields such as medical, technical, legal and _____.
   a. Hypernorms
   b. Corporate Sustainability
   c. Facilitation payments
   d. Business ethics

2. An _____ is a situation that will often involve an apparent conflict between moral imperatives, in which to obey one would result in transgressing another. This is also called an ethical paradox since in moral philosophy, paradox plays a central role in ethics debates. For instance, an ethical admonition to 'love thy neighbour as thy self' is not always just in contrast with, but sometimes in contradiction to an armed neighbour actively trying to kill you: if he or she succeeds, you will not be able to love him or her.
   a. A4e
   b. Ethical dilemma
   c. AAAI
   d. A Stake in the Outcome

3. _____ is the conduct of a trustee, an attorney, a corporate officer corporate shareholders, or his clients. _____ may involve misappropriation or usurpation of corporate assets or opportunities.

One of the more current and widely agreed on definitions is from political scientists Ken Kernaghan and John Langford in their book 'The Responsible Public Servant'.

   a. Letter of credit
   b. Certificate of Incorporation
   c. Financial Security Law of France
   d. Self-dealing

4. _____ can be regarded as an outcome of mental processes (cognitive process) leading to the selection of a course of action among several alternatives. Every _____ process produces a final choice. The output can be an action or an opinion of choice.
   a. 1990 Clean Air Act
   b. 28-hour day
   c. Decision making
   d. 33 Strategies of War

5. _____ is an idea in the field of Organizational studies and management which describes the psychology, attitudes, experiences, beliefs and Values (personal and cultural values) of an organization. It has been defined as 'the specific collection of values and norms that are shared by people and groups in an organization and that control the way they interact with each other and with stakeholders outside the organization.'

This definition continues to explain organizational values also known as 'beliefs and ideas about what kinds of goals members of an organization should pursue and ideas about the appropriate kinds or standards of behavior organizational members should use to achieve these goals. From organizational values develop organizational norms, guidelines or expectations that prescribe appropriate kinds of behavior by employees in particular situations and control the behavior of organizational members towards one another.'

_____ is not the same as corporate culture.

a. Organizational culture
b. Organizational development
c. Union shop
d. Organizational effectiveness

6. _____ is the set of processes, customs, policies, laws, and institutions affecting the way a corporation (or company) is directed, administered or controlled. _____ also includes the relationships among the many stakeholders involved and the goals for which the corporation is governed. The principal stakeholders are the shareholders/members, management, and the board of directors.
a. Flextime
b. Guarantee
c. No-FEAR Act
d. Corporate governance

7. The _____ of 2002 (Pub.L. 107-204, 116 Stat. 745, enacted July 30, 2002), also known as the Public Company Accounting Reform and Investor Protection Act of 2002 and commonly called Sarbanes-Oxley, Sarbox or SOX, is a United States federal law enacted on July 30, 2002, as a reaction to a number of major corporate and accounting scandals including those affecting Enron, Tyco International, Adelphia, Peregrine Systems and WorldCom.
a. Fair Labor Standards Act
b. Letter of credit
c. Sarbanes-Oxley Act of 2002
d. Sarbanes-Oxley Act

8. The _____ is an idea proposed by economic theorist Milton Friedman, which states that a company's only responsibility is to increase its profits.

Chapter 4. Stakeholders, Ethics, and Corporate Social Responsibility

Friedman argued that a company should have no 'social responsibility' to the public or society because its only concern is to increase profits for itself and for its shareholders. He wrote about this concept in his book Capitalism and Freedom.

a. 33 Strategies of War
b. 1990 Clean Air Act
c. 28-hour day
d. Friedman doctrine

Chapter 5. Planning and Decision Making

1. _____ is an organization's process of defining its strategy and making decisions on allocating its resources to pursue this strategy, including its capital and people. Various business analysis techniques can be used in _____, including SWOT analysis (Strengths, Weaknesses, Opportunities, and Threats) and PEST analysis (Political, Economic, Social, and Technological analysis) or STEER analysis involving Socio-cultural, Technological, Economic, Ecological, and Regulatory factors and EPISTEL (Environment, Political, Informatic, Social, Technological, Economic and Legal)

_____ is the formal consideration of an organization's future course. All _____ deals with at least one of three key questions:

1. 'What do we do?'
2. 'For whom do we do it?'
3. 'How do we excel?'

In business _____, the third question is better phrased 'How can we beat or avoid competition?'. (Bradford and Duncan, page 1.)

   a. 33 Strategies of War
   b. Strategic planning
   c. 1990 Clean Air Act
   d. 28-hour day

2. The _____ is the amount of time an organization will look into the future when preparing a strategic plan. Many commercial companies use a five-year _____, but other organizations such as the Forestry Commission in the UK have to use a much longer _____ to form effective plans.
   a. No-bid contract
   b. Psychological pricing
   c. Planning horizon
   d. Strategic Alliance

3. A _____ is a plan devised for a specific situation when things could go wrong. _____s are often devised by governments or businesses who want to be prepared for anything that could happen. They are sometimes known as 'Back-up plans', 'Worst-case scenario plans' or 'Plan B'.
   a. 28-hour day
   b. 1990 Clean Air Act
   c. 33 Strategies of War
   d. Contingency plan

4. _____ is the process by which an organization deals with any major unpredictable event that threatens to harm the organization, its stakeholders, or the general public. Three elements are common to most definitions of crisis: (a) a threat to the organization, (b) the element of surprise, and (c) a short decision time.

Chapter 5. Planning and Decision Making

Whereas risk management involves assessing potential threats and finding the best ways to avoid those threats, _____ involves dealing with the disasters after they have occurred.

a. C-A-K-E
b. Capability management
c. Business value
d. Crisis management

5. Network externalities resemble economies of scale, but they are not considered such because they are a function of the number of users of a good or service in an industry, not of the production efficiency within a business. _____ are only considered examples of network externalities if they are driven by demand side economies.

Formally, a production function is defined to have:

- constant returns to scale if (for any constant a greater than or equal to 0)
- increasing returns to scale if (for any constant a greater than 1)
- decreasing returns to scale if (for any constant a greater than 1)

where K and L are factors of production, capital and labour, respectively.

As an example, the Cobb-Douglas functional form has constant returns to scale when the sum of the exponents adds up to one.

a. A4e
b. A Stake in the Outcome
c. AAAI
d. Economies of scale external to the firm

6. _____ is a strategic planning method used to evaluate the Strengths, Weaknesses, Opportunities, and Threats involved in a project or in a business venture. It involves specifying the objective of the business venture or project and identifying the internal and external factors that are favorable and unfavorable to achieving that objective. The technique is credited to Albert Humphrey, who led a convention at Stanford University in the 1960s and 1970s using data from Fortune 500 companies.

a. Marketing
b. Market share
c. SWOT analysis
d. Corporate image

7. The _____ is a performance management tool for measuring whether the smaller-scale operational activities of a company are aligned with its larger-scale objectives in terms of vision and strategy.

By focusing not only on financial outcomes but also on the operational, marketing and developmental inputs to these, the _____ helps provide a more comprehensive view of a business, which in turn helps organizations act in their best long-term interests. This tool is also being used to address business response to climate change and greenhouse gas emissions.

a. Middle management
b. Commercial management
c. Management development
d. Balanced scorecard

8. _____ can be regarded as an outcome of mental processes (cognitive process) leading to the selection of a course of action among several alternatives. Every _____ process produces a final choice. The output can be an action or an opinion of choice.
a. Decision making
b. 1990 Clean Air Act
c. 33 Strategies of War
d. 28-hour day

9. _____ is a concept based on the fact that rationality of individuals is limited by the information they have, the cognitive limitations of their minds, and the finite amount of time they have to make decisions. This contrasts with the concept of rationality as optimization. Another way to look at _____ is that, because decision-makers lack the ability and resources to arrive at the optimal solution, they instead apply their rationality only after having greatly simplified the choices available.
a. Mixed strategy
b. Complete information
c. Transferable utility
d. Bounded rationality

Chapter 5. Planning and Decision Making

10. A _____ is a person's tendency to make errors in judgment based on cognitive factors, and is a phenomenon studied in cognitive science and social psychology. Forms of _____ include errors in statistical judgment, social attribution, and memory that are common to all human beings. Such biases drastically skew the reliability of anecdotal and legal evidence.
    a. Cognitive dissonance
    b. Cognitive bias
    c. Psychological statistics
    d. Diffusion of responsibility

11. A cognitive bias is a pattern of deviation in judgment that occurs in particular situations Implicit in the concept of a 'pattern of deviation' is a standard of comparison; this may be the judgment of people outside those particular situations, or may be a set of independently verifiable facts. The existence of some of these _____ has been verified empirically in the field of psychology, others are widespread beliefs, and may themselves be a consequence of cognitive bias.
    a. Halo effect
    b. Choice-supportive bias
    c. Distinction bias
    d. Cognitive biases

12. _____ is an adjective for experience-based techniques that help in problem solving, learning and discovery. A _____ method is particularly used to rapidly come to a solution that is hoped to be close to the best possible answer, or 'optimal solution'. _____s are 'rules of thumb', educated guesses, intuitive judgments or simply common sense.
    a. 28-hour day
    b. 1990 Clean Air Act
    c. Representativeness
    d. Heuristic

13. _____ is one of the managerial functions like planning, organizing, staffing and directing. It is an important function because it helps to check the errors and to take the corrective action so that deviation from standards are minimized and stated goals of the organization are achieved in desired manner. According to modern concepts, _____ is a foreseeing action whereas earlier concept of _____ was used only when errors were detected. _____ in management means setting standards, measuring actual performance and taking corrective action.
    a. Turnover
    b. Decision tree pruning
    c. Schedule of reinforcement
    d. Control

14. The _____ heuristic is a heuristic wherein people assume commonality between objects of similar appearance, or between an object and a group it appears to fit into. While often very useful in everyday life, it can also result in neglect of relevant base rates and other cognitive biases. The representative heuristic was first proposed by Amos Tversky and Daniel Kahneman.
   a. Representativeness
   b. Representativeness heuristic
   c. 28-hour day
   d. 1990 Clean Air Act

15. _____ is a theory that describes decisions between alternatives that involve risk, i.e. alternatives with uncertain outcomes, where the probabilities are known. The model is descriptive: it tries to model real-life choices, rather than optimal decisions.

_____ was developed by Daniel Kahneman, professor at Princeton University's Department of Psychology, and Amos Tversky in 1979 as a psychologically realistic alternative to expected utility theory.

   a. Mental accounting
   b. Loss aversion
   c. Prospect theory
   d. 1990 Clean Air Act

16. _____ is a type of thought exhibited by group members who try to minimize conflict and reach consensus without critically testing, analyzing, and evaluating ideas. Individual creativity, uniqueness, and independent thinking are lost in the pursuit of group cohesiveness, as are the advantages of reasonable balance in choice and thought that might normally be obtained by making decisions as a group. During _____, members of the group avoid promoting viewpoints outside the comfort zone of consensus thinking.
   a. Diffusion of responsibility
   b. Psychological statistics
   c. Groupthink
   d. Self-report inventory

17. _____ is the pursuit of influencing outcomes -- including public-policy and resource allocation decisions within political, economic, and social systems and institutions -- that directly affect people's current lives. (Cohen, 2001)

Therefore, _____ can be seen as a deliberate process of speaking out on issues of concern in order to exert some influence on behalf of ideas or persons. Based on this definition, Cohen (2001) states that 'ideologues of all persuasions advocate' to bring a change in people's lives.

a. AAAI
b. A4e
c. A Stake in the Outcome
d. Advocacy

Chapter 6. Strategy

1. _____ is, in very basic words, a position a firm occupies against its competitors.

According to Michael Porter, the three methods for creating a sustainable _____ are through:

1. Cost leadership

2. Differentiation

3. Focus (economics)

  a. 28-hour day
  b. 1990 Clean Air Act
  c. Theory Z
  d. Competitive advantage

2. Competitive advantage is, in very basic words, a position a firm occupies against its competitors.

According to Michael Porter, the three methods for creating a _____ are through:

1. Cost leadership - Cost advantage occurs when a firm delivers the same services as its competitors but at a lower cost;

2.

  a. Sustainable competitive advantage
  b. Theory Z
  c. 28-hour day
  d. 1990 Clean Air Act

3. _____, in microeconomics, are the cost advantages that a business obtains due to expansion. They are factors that cause a producer's average cost per unit to fall as scale is increased. _____ is a long run concept and refers to reductions in unit cost as the size of a facility, or scale, increases.
  a. Economies of scope
  b. A4e
  c. A Stake in the Outcome
  d. Economies of scale

Chapter 6. Strategy

4. A _____ is a group of people or organizations sharing one or more characteristics that cause them to have similar product and/or service needs. A true _____ meets all of the following criteria: it is distinct from other segments (different segments have different needs), it is homogeneous within the segment (exhibits common needs); it responds similarly to a market stimulus, and it can be reached by a market intervention. The term is also used when consumers with identical product and/or service needs are divided up into groups so they can be charged different amounts.

   a. SWOT analysis
   b. Customer relationship management
   c. Context analysis
   d. Market segment

5. A _____ is a process that can allow an organization to concentrate its limited resources on the greatest opportunities to increase sales and achieve a sustainable competitive advantage. A _____ should be centered around the key concept that customer satisfaction is the main goal.

   A _____ is a written plan which combines product development, promotion, distribution, and pricing approach, identifies the firm's marketing goals, and explains how they will be achieved within a stated timeframe.

   a. Product bundling
   b. Disruptive technology
   c. Category management
   d. Marketing strategy

6. In economics, _____ refers to how the marginal contribution of a factor of production usually decreases as more of the factor is used. According to this relationship, in a production system with fixed and variable inputs, beyond some point, each additional unit of the variable input yields smaller and smaller increases in output. Conversely, producing one more unit of output costs more and more in variable inputs.

   a. Federal Employers Liability Act
   b. Diminishing returns
   c. Negligence
   d. Blue sky law

7. _____ is an integrated communications-based process through which individuals and communities discover that existing and newly-identified needs and wants may be satisfied by the products and services of others.

   _____ is defined by the American _____ Association as the activity, set of institutions, and processes for creating, communicating, delivering, and exchanging offerings that have value for customers, clients, partners, and society at large. The term developed from the original meaning which referred literally to going to market, as in shopping, or going to a market to buy or sell goods or services.

a. Customer relationship management
b. Disruptive technology
c. Market development
d. Marketing

8. The phrase _____, according to the Organization for Economic Co-operation and Development, refers to 'creative work undertaken on a systematic basis in order to increase the stock of knowledge, including knowledge of man, culture and society, and the use of this stock of knowledge to devise new applications [sic]'

New product design and development is more than often a crucial factor in the survival of a company. In an industry that is fast changing, firms must continually revise their design and range of products. This is necessary due to continuous technology change and development as well as other competitors and the changing preference of customers.

a. 1990 Clean Air Act
b. 28-hour day
c. 33 Strategies of War
d. Research and development

9. The _____ is a concept from business management that was first described and popularized by Michael Porter in his 1985 best-seller, Competitive Advantage: Creating and Sustaining Superior Performance.

A _____ is a chain of activities. Products pass through all activities of the chain in order and at each activity the product gains some value. The chain of activities gives the products more added value than the sum of added values of all activities. It is important not to mix the concept of the _____ with the costs occurring throughout the activities.

a. Value chain
b. Customer relationship management
c. Mass marketing
d. Market development

10. _____ in its literal sense is the process of transformation of local or regional phenomena into global ones. It can be described as a process by which the people of the world are unified into a single society and function together.

This process is a combination of economic, technological, sociocultural and political forces.

Chapter 6. Strategy

   a. Cost Management
   b. Histogram
   c. Globalization
   d. Collaborative Planning, Forecasting and Replenishment

11. _____ is an increasingly broadening term with which an organization, or other human system describes the combination of traditionally administrative personnel functions with acquisition and application of skills, knowledge and experience, Employee Relations and resource planning at various levels. The field draws upon concepts developed in Industrial/Organizational Psychology and System Theory. _____ has at least two related interpretations depending on context. The original usage derives from political economy and economics, where it was traditionally called labor, one of four factors of production although this perspective is changing as a function of new and ongoing research into more strategic approaches at national levels. This first usage is used more in terms of '_____ development', and can go beyond just organizations to the level of nations . The more traditional usage within corporations and businesses refers to the individuals within a firm or agency, and to the portion of the organization that deals with hiring, firing, training, and other personnel issues, typically referred to as `_____ management'.
   a. Human resource management
   b. Progressive discipline
   c. Human resources
   d. Bradford Factor

12. _____ is the acquisition of goods and/or services at the best possible total cost of ownership, in the right quality and quantity, at the right time, in the right place and from the right source for the direct benefit or use of corporations, individuals generally via a contract. Simple _____ may involve nothing more than repeat purchasing. Complex _____ could involve finding long term partners - or even 'co-destiny' suppliers that might fundamentally commit one organization to another.
   a. Psychological pricing
   b. Sole proprietorship
   c. Golden parachute
   d. Procurement

13. _____ is an advertisement in which a particular product specifically mentions a competitor by name for the express purpose of showing why the competitor is inferior to the product naming it.

This should not be confused with parody advertisements, where a fictional product is being advertised for the purpose of poking fun at the particular advertisement, nor should it be confused with the use of a coined brand name for the purpose of comparing the product without actually naming an actual competitor. ('Wikipedia tastes better and is less filling than the Encyclopedia Galactica.')

In the 1980s, during what has been referred to as the cola wars, soft-drink manufacturer Pepsi ran a series of advertisements where people, caught on hidden camera, in a blind taste test, chose Pepsi over rival Coca-Cola.

a. 1990 Clean Air Act
b. 33 Strategies of War
c. 28-hour day
d. Comparative advertising

14. _____ is one of the managerial functions like planning, organizing, staffing and directing. It is an important function because it helps to check the errors and to take the corrective action so that deviation from standards are minimized and stated goals of the organization are achieved in desired manner. According to modern concepts, _____ is a foreseeing action whereas earlier concept of _____ was used only when errors were detected. _____ in management means setting standards, measuring actual performance and taking corrective action.
   a. Control
   b. Schedule of reinforcement
   c. Decision tree pruning
   d. Turnover

15. In economics and sociology, an _____ is any factor (financial or non-financial) that enables or motivates a particular course of action, or counts as a reason for preferring one choice to the alternatives. It is an expectation that encourages people to behave in a certain way. Since human beings are purposeful creatures, the study of _____ structures is central to the study of all economic activity (both in terms of individual decision-making and in terms of co-operation and competition within a larger institutional structure.)
   a. A Stake in the Outcome
   b. AAAI
   c. A4e
   d. Incentive

16. _____ is an idea in the field of Organizational studies and management which describes the psychology, attitudes, experiences, beliefs and Values (personal and cultural values) of an organization. It has been defined as 'the specific collection of values and norms that are shared by people and groups in an organization and that control the way they interact with each other and with stakeholders outside the organization.'

This definition continues to explain organizational values also known as 'beliefs and ideas about what kinds of goals members of an organization should pursue and ideas about the appropriate kinds or standards of behavior organizational members should use to achieve these goals. From organizational values develop organizational norms, guidelines or expectations that prescribe appropriate kinds of behavior by employees in particular situations and control the behavior of organizational members towards one another.'

_____ is not the same as corporate culture.

a. Organizational culture
b. Union shop
c. Organizational effectiveness
d. Organizational development

17. _____ is one of the four Ps of the marketing mix. The other three aspects are product, promotion, and place. It is also a key variable in microeconomic price allocation theory.
  a. Transfer pricing
  b. Price floor
  c. Penetration pricing
  d. Pricing

18. In microeconomics and management, the term _____ describes a style of management control. Vertically integrated companies are united through a hierarchy with a common owner. Usually each member of the hierarchy produces a different product or (market-specific) service, and the products combine to satisfy a common need.
  a. 33 Strategies of War
  b. 28-hour day
  c. 1990 Clean Air Act
  d. Vertical integration

19. _____ is something that a firm can do well and that meets the following three conditions:

Competencies are things that companys execute well across several business units or product sectors.

Firms usually have few competencies, but these are usually less liable to change rapidly.

  1. It provides consumer benefits
  2. It is not easy for competitors to imitate
  3. It can be leveraged widely to many products and markets.

A _____ can take various forms, including technical/subject matter know-how, a reliable process and/or close relationships with customers and suppliers (Mascarenhas et al. 1998.)

  a. Core competency
  b. Learning-by-doing
  c. NAIRU
  d. Dominant Design

20. _____ are conceptually similar to economies of scale. Whereas economies of scale primarily refer to efficiencies associated with supply-side changes, such as increasing or decreasing the scale of production, of a single product type, _____ refer to efficiencies primarily associated with demand-side changes, such as increasing or decreasing the scope of marketing and distribution, of different types of products. _____ are one of the main reasons for such marketing strategies as product bundling, product lining, and family branding.

a. A Stake in the Outcome
b. A4e
c. Economies of scale
d. Economies of scope

Chapter 7. Managing Operations

1. _____ refers to metrics and measures of output from production processes, per unit of input. Labor _____, for example, is typically measured as a ratio of output per labor-hour, an input. _____ may be conceived of as a metrics of the technical or engineering efficiency of production.
   a. Productivity
   b. Remanufacturing
   c. Master production schedule
   d. Value engineering

2. _____ is the amount of goods and services that a labourer produces in a given amount of time. It is one of several types of productivity that economists measure. _____ can be measured for a firm, a process or a country.
   a. Time and attendance
   b. Labour productivity
   c. Retroactive overtime
   d. Business Network Transformation

3. A _____ is a computer program typically used to provide some form of artificial intelligence, which consists primarily of a set of rules about behavior. These rules, termed productions, are a basic representation found useful in AI planning, expert systems and action selection. A _____ provides the mechanism necessary to execute productions in order to achieve some goal for the system.
   a. 33 Strategies of War
   b. 1990 Clean Air Act
   c. 28-hour day
   d. Production system

4. In probability theory, a probability distribution is called _____ if its cumulative distribution function is _____. This is equivalent to saying that for random variables X with the distribution in question, Pr[X = a] = 0 for all real numbers a, i.e.: the probability that X attains the value a is zero, for any number a. If the distribution of X is _____ then X is called a _____ random variable.
   a. Pay Band
   b. Decision tree pruning
   c. Connectionist expert systems
   d. Continuous

5. In economics, business, retail, and accounting, a _____ is the value of money that has been used up to produce something, and hence is not available for use anymore. In economics, a _____ is an alternative that is given up as a result of a decision. In business, the _____ may be one of acquisition, in which case the amount of money expended to acquire it is counted as _____.

Chapter 7. Managing Operations

a. Cost allocation
b. Cost
c. Cost overrun
d. Fixed costs

6. _____, in microeconomics, are the cost advantages that a business obtains due to expansion. They are factors that cause a producer's average cost per unit to fall as scale is increased. _____ is a long run concept and refers to reductions in unit cost as the size of a facility, or scale, increases.

a. A4e
b. A Stake in the Outcome
c. Economies of scope
d. Economies of scale

7. _____ is the production of large amounts of standardized products, including and especially on assembly lines. The concepts of _____ are applied to various kinds of products, from fluids and particulates handled in bulk to discrete solid parts to assemblies of such parts

_____ of assemblies typically uses electric-motor-powered moving tracks or conveyor belts to move partially complete products to workers, who perform simple repetitive tasks.

a. 1990 Clean Air Act
b. Mass production
c. 33 Strategies of War
d. 28-hour day

8. _____, in marketing, manufacturing, call centres and management, is the use of flexible computer-aided manufacturing systems to produce custom output. Those systems combine the low unit costs of mass production processes with the flexibility of individual customization.

'_____' is the new frontier in business competition for both manufacturing and service industries.

a. 33 Strategies of War
b. Mass customization
c. 1990 Clean Air Act
d. 28-hour day

Chapter 7. Managing Operations

9. In business and accounting, _____s are everything of value that is owned by a person or company. Any property or object of value that one possesses, usually considered as applicable to the payment of one's debts is considered an _____. Simplistically stated, _____s are things of value that can be readily converted into cash.
   a. A4e
   b. Asset
   c. A Stake in the Outcome
   d. AAAI

10. In queueing theory, _____ is the proportion of the system's resources which is used by the traffic which arrives at it. It should be strictly less than one for the system to function well. It is usually represented by the symbol ρ.
    a. A4e
    b. AAAI
    c. Utilization
    d. A Stake in the Outcome

11. _____ can be considered to have three main components: quality control, quality assurance and quality improvement. _____ is focused not only on product quality, but also the means to achieve it. _____ therefore uses quality assurance and control of processes as well as products to achieve more consistent quality.
    a. 1990 Clean Air Act
    b. 28-hour day
    c. Total quality management
    d. Quality management

12. The 'business case for _____', theorizes that in a global marketplace, a company that employs a diverse workforce (both men and women, people of many generations, people from ethnically and racially diverse backgrounds etc.) is better able to understand the demographics of the marketplace it serves and is thus better equipped to thrive in that marketplace than a company that has a more limited range of employee demographics.

    An additional corollary suggests that a company that supports the _____ of its workforce can also improve employee satisfaction, productivity and retention.

    a. Virtual team
    b. Trademark
    c. Kanban
    d. Diversity

13. _____ is a business management strategy, initially implemented by Motorola, that today enjoys widespread application in many sectors of industry.

_____ seeks to improve the quality of process outputs by identifying and removing the causes of defects (errors) and variation in manufacturing and business processes. It uses a set of quality management methods, including statistical methods, and creates a special infrastructure of people within the organization ('Black Belts' etc.)

  a. Takt time
  b. Production line
  c. Six sigma
  d. Theory of constraints

14. _____ is a business management strategy aimed at embedding awareness of quality in all organizational processes. _____ has been widely used in manufacturing, education, hospitals, call centers, government, and service industries, as well as NASA space and science programs.

As defined by the International Organization for Standardization (ISO):

'_____ is a management approach for an organization, centered on quality, based on the participation of all its members and aiming at long-term success through customer satisfaction, and benefits to all members of the organization and to society.' ISO 8402:1994

One major aim is to reduce variation from every process so that greater consistency of effort is obtained. (Royse, D., Thyer, B., Padgett D., ' Logan T., 2006)

  a. Quality management
  b. 28-hour day
  c. 1990 Clean Air Act
  d. Total quality management

15. _____ is the state of being which occurs when a person, object, or service is no longer wanted even though it may still be in good working order. _____ frequently occurs because a replacement has become available that is superior in one or more aspects. Videotapes making way for DVDs

Technical _____ may occur when a new product or technology supersedes the old, and it becomes preferred to utilize the new technology in place of the old.

Chapter 7. Managing Operations

a. A Stake in the Outcome
b. A4e
c. Obsolescence
d. AAAI

16. _____ is a reduction in the value of a currency with respect to other monetary units. In common modern usage, it specifically implies an official lowering of the value of a country's currency within a fixed exchange rate system, by which the monetary authority formally sets a new fixed rate with respect to a foreign reference currency. In contrast, depreciation is used for the unofficial decrease in the exchange rate in a floating exchange rate system.

a. 33 Strategies of War
b. 1990 Clean Air Act
c. 28-hour day
d. Devaluation

17. In business management, _____ is money spent to keep and maintain a stock of goods in storage.

The most obvious _____s include rent for the required space; equipment, materials, and labor to operate the space; insurance; security; interest on money invested in the inventory and space, and other direct expenses. Some stored goods become obsolete before they are sold, reducing their contribution to revenue while having no effect on their _____.

a. Private placement
b. Choquet integral
c. Market niche
d. Holding cost

18. _____ is the level of inventory that minimizes the total inventory holding costs and ordering costs. The framework used to determine this order quantity is also known as Wilson _____ Model. The model was developed by F. W. Harris in 1913.

a. Effective executive
b. Anti-leadership
c. Event management
d. Economic order quantity

19. The _____ is an equation that equals the cost of goods sold divided by the average inventory. Average inventory equals beginning inventory plus ending inventory divided by 2.

Chapter 7. Managing Operations

The formula for _____:

>

The formula for average inventory:

>

A low turnover rate may point to overstocking, obsolescence, or deficiencies in the product line or marketing effort.

a. Asset turnover
b. A Stake in the Outcome
c. A4e
d. Inventory turnover

20. _____ is an inventory strategy that strives to improve the return on investment of a business by reducing in-process inventory and its associated carrying costs. To meet _____ objectives, the process relies on signals between different points in the process. This means the process is often driven by a series of signals, or Kanban, which tell production when to make the next part. Kanban are usually 'tickets' but can be simple visual signals, such as the presence or absence of a part on a shelf. Implemented correctly, _____ can dramatically improve a manufacturing organization's return on investment, quality, and efficiency.

a. 33 Strategies of War
b. 1990 Clean Air Act
c. Just-in-time
d. 28-hour day

21. In a human resources context, _____ or labor _____ is the rate at which an employer gains and loses employees. Simple ways to describe it are 'how long employees tend to stay' or 'the rate of traffic through the revolving door.' _____ is measured for individual companies and for their industry as a whole. If an employer is said to have a high _____ relative to its competitors, it means that employees of that company have a shorter average tenure than those of other companies in the same industry.

a. Ten year occupational employment projection
b. Continuous
c. Turnover
d. Career portfolios

Chapter 7. Managing Operations
45

22. _____ is a concept related to lean and just-in-time (JIT) production. The Japanese word _____ is a common term meaning 'signboard' or 'billboard'. According to Taiichi Ohno, the man credited with developing JIT, _____ is a means through which JIT is achieved.
   a. Trademark
   b. Succession planning
   c. Risk management
   d. Kanban

23. The '_____ scheme' is an economic term, referring to the use of commodity storage for economic stabilization. Specifically, commodities are bought and stored when there is a surplus in the economy and they are sold from these stores when there are shortages in the economy. The institutional buying, storing and selling of commodities by a large player (e.g. a government) can take place for one commodity or a 'basket of commodities'.
   a. Reservation wage
   b. Buffer stock
   c. Contingent employment
   d. Power

24. _____ refers to the structured transmission of data between organizations by electronic means. It is used to transfer electronic documents from one computer system to another (ie) from one trading partner to another trading partner. It is more than mere E-mail; for instance, organizations might replace bills of lading and even checks with appropriate _____ messages.
   a. A Stake in the Outcome
   b. A4e
   c. Electronic data interchange
   d. AAAI

25. A _____ is the system of organizations, people, technology, activities, information and resources involved in moving a product or service from supplier to customer. _____ activities transform natural resources, raw materials and components into a finished product that is delivered to the end customer. In sophisticated _____ systems, used products may re-enter the _____ at any point where residual value is recyclable.
   a. Packaging
   b. Wholesalers
   c. Drop shipping
   d. Supply chain

26. _____ is the management of a network of interconnected businesses involved in the ultimate provision of product and service packages required by end customers (Harland, 1996.) _____ spans all movement and storage of raw materials, work-in-process inventory, and finished goods from point of origin to point of consumption (supply chain.)

Chapter 7. Managing Operations

The definition an American professional association put forward is that _____ encompasses the planning and management of all activities involved in sourcing, procurement, conversion, and logistics management activities.

a. Drop shipping
b. Freight forwarder
c. Packaging
d. Supply chain management

27. In business and engineering, new _____ is the term used to describe the complete process of bringing a new product or service to market. There are two parallel paths involved in the NProduct development process: one involves the idea generation, product design, and detail engineering; the other involves market research and marketing analysis. Companies typically see new _____ as the first stage in generating and commercializing new products within the overall strategic process of product life cycle management used to maintain or grow their market share.

a. 1990 Clean Air Act
b. 33 Strategies of War
c. 28-hour day
d. Product development

28. The phrase _____, according to the Organization for Economic Co-operation and Development, refers to 'creative work undertaken on a systematic basis in order to increase the stock of knowledge, including knowledge of man, culture and society, and the use of this stock of knowledge to devise new applications [sic]'

New product design and development is more than often a crucial factor in the survival of a company. In an industry that is fast changing, firms must continually revise their design and range of products. This is necessary due to continuous technology change and development as well as other competitors and the changing preference of customers.

a. Research and development
b. 1990 Clean Air Act
c. 33 Strategies of War
d. 28-hour day

Chapter 8. Organizing

1. _____ is one of the managerial functions like planning, organizing, staffing and directing. It is an important function because it helps to check the errors and to take the corrective action so that deviation from standards are minimized and stated goals of the organization are achieved in desired manner.According to modern concepts, _____ is a foreseeing action whereas earlier concept of _____ was used only when errors were detected. _____ in management means setting standards, measuring actual performance and taking corrective action.
    a. Turnover
    b. Schedule of reinforcement
    c. Control
    d. Decision tree pruning

2. In economics and sociology, an _____ is any factor (financial or non-financial) that enables or motivates a particular course of action, or counts as a reason for preferring one choice to the alternatives. It is an expectation that encourages people to behave in a certain way. Since human beings are purposeful creatures, the study of _____ structures is central to the study of all economic activity (both in terms of individual decision-making and in terms of co-operation and competition within a larger institutional structure.)
    a. A Stake in the Outcome
    b. AAAI
    c. A4e
    d. Incentive

3. _____ is an idea in the field of Organizational studies and management which describes the psychology, attitudes, experiences, beliefs and Values (personal and cultural values) of an organization. It has been defined as 'the specific collection of values and norms that are shared by people and groups in an organization and that control the way they interact with each other and with stakeholders outside the organization.'

This definition continues to explain organizational values also known as 'beliefs and ideas about what kinds of goals members of an organization should pursue and ideas about the appropriate kinds or standards of behavior organizational members should use to achieve these goals. From organizational values develop organizational norms, guidelines or expectations that prescribe appropriate kinds of behavior by employees in particular situations and control the behavior of organizational members towards one another.'

_____ is not the same as corporate culture.

   a. Union shop
   b. Organizational development
   c. Organizational effectiveness
   d. Organizational culture

4. _____ is the process by which the activities of an organisation, particularly those regarding decision-making, become concentrated within a particular location and/or group.

a. Chief operating officer
b. Product innovation
c. Corner office
d. Centralization

5. _____ is the process of dispersing decision-making governance closer to the people or citizen. It includes the dispersal of administration or governance in sectors or areas like engineering, management science, political science, political economy, sociology and economics. _____ is also possible in the dispersal of population and employment.

a. Formula for Change
b. Decentralization
c. Business plan
d. Frenemy

6. _____ consists of the mental process of thinking involved with the process of judging the merits of multiple options and selecting one of them for action. Some simple examples include deciding whether to get up in the morning or go back to sleep, or selecting a given route for a journey. More complex examples (often decisions that affect what a person thinks or their core beliefs) include choosing a lifestyle, religious affiliation, or political position.

a. Championship mobilization
b. Groups decision making
c. Trade study
d. Choice

7. _____ is a term originating in military organization theory, but now used more commonly in business management, particularly human resource management. _____ refers to the number of subordinates a supervisor has.

In the hierarchical business organization of the past it was not uncommon to see average spans of 1 to 10 or even less. That is, one manager supervised ten employees on average.

a. CIFMS
b. Senior management
c. Mentoring
d. Span of control

8. In economics, business, retail, and accounting, a _____ is the value of money that has been used up to produce something, and hence is not available for use anymore. In economics, a _____ is an alternative that is given up as a result of a decision. In business, the _____ may be one of acquisition, in which case the amount of money expended to acquire it is counted as _____.

a. Cost allocation
b. Cost
c. Fixed costs
d. Cost overrun

9. _____ is a term in management and corporate restructuring that refers to a planned reduction in the number of layers of a management hierarchy.
   a. Mass market
   b. Delayering
   c. Product innovation
   d. Supervisory board

Chapter 9. Control Systems

1. _____ is one of the managerial functions like planning, organizing, staffing and directing. It is an important function because it helps to check the errors and to take the corrective action so that deviation from standards are minimized and stated goals of the organization are achieved in desired manner. According to modern concepts, _____ is a foreseeing action whereas earlier concept of _____ was used only when errors were detected. _____ in management means setting standards, measuring actual performance and taking corrective action.
   a. Turnover
   b. Control
   c. Schedule of reinforcement
   d. Decision tree pruning

2. A _____ is a change implemented to address a weakness identified in a management system. Normally _____s are implemented in response to a customer complaint, abnormal levels of internal nonconformity, nonconformities identified during an internal audit or adverse or unstable trends in product and process monitoring such as would be identified by SPC.

   The process of determining a _____ requires identification of actions that can be taken to prevent or mitigate the weakness.

   a. Zero defects
   b. 1990 Clean Air Act
   c. Corrective action
   d. 28-hour day

3. In operant conditioning, _____ occurs when an event following a response causes an increase in the probability of that response occurring in the future. Response strength can be assessed by measures such as the frequency with which the response is made (for example, a pigeon may peck a key more times in the session), or the speed with which it is made (for example, a rat may run a maze faster.) The environment change contingent upon the response is called a reinforcer.
   a. Historiometry
   b. Meetings, Incentives, Conferences, and Exhibitions
   c. Diminishing Manufacturing Sources and Material Shortages
   d. Reinforcement

4. In economics and sociology, an _____ is any factor (financial or non-financial) that enables or motivates a particular course of action, or counts as a reason for preferring one choice to the alternatives. It is an expectation that encourages people to behave in a certain way. Since human beings are purposeful creatures, the study of _____ structures is central to the study of all economic activity (both in terms of individual decision-making and in terms of co-operation and competition within a larger institutional structure.)

Chapter 9. Control Systems

a. AAAI
b. A Stake in the Outcome
c. Incentive
d. A4e

5. A _____ is a process in which a potential employee is evaluated by an employer for prospective employment in their company, organization and was established in the late 16th century.

A _____ typically precedes the hiring decision, and is used to evaluate the candidate. The interview is usually preceded by the evaluation of submitted résumés from interested candidates, then selecting a small number of candidates for interviews.

a. Split shift
b. Payrolling
c. Supported employment
d. Job interview

6. The _____ is a performance management tool for measuring whether the smaller-scale operational activities of a company are aligned with its larger-scale objectives in terms of vision and strategy.

By focusing not only on financial outcomes but also on the operational, marketing and developmental inputs to these, the _____ helps provide a more comprehensive view of a business, which in turn helps organizations act in their best long-term interests. This tool is also being used to address business response to climate change and greenhouse gas emissions.

a. Management development
b. Commercial management
c. Middle management
d. Balanced scorecard

Chapter 10. Organizational Culture

1. _____ is an idea in the field of Organizational studies and management which describes the psychology, attitudes, experiences, beliefs and Values (personal and cultural values) of an organization. It has been defined as 'the specific collection of values and norms that are shared by people and groups in an organization and that control the way they interact with each other and with stakeholders outside the organization.'

This definition continues to explain organizational values also known as 'beliefs and ideas about what kinds of goals members of an organization should pursue and ideas about the appropriate kinds or standards of behavior organizational members should use to achieve these goals. From organizational values develop organizational norms, guidelines or expectations that prescribe appropriate kinds of behavior by employees in particular situations and control the behavior of organizational members towards one another.'

_____ is not the same as corporate culture.

 a. Union shop
 b. Organizational culture
 c. Organizational effectiveness
 d. Organizational development

2. Organizational culture is not the same as _____. It is wider and deeper concepts, something that an organization 'is' rather than what it 'has' (according to Buchanan and Huczynski.)

_____ is the total sum of the values, customs, traditions and meanings that make a company unique.

 a. Job analysis
 b. Work design
 c. Path-goal theory
 d. Corporate culture

3. In sociology, anthropology and cultural studies, a _____ is a group of people with a culture (whether distinct or hidden) which differentiates them from the larger culture to which they belong. If a particular _____ is characterized by a systematic opposition to the dominant culture, it may be described as a counterculture.

As early as 1950, David Riesman distinguished between a majority, 'which passively accepted commercially provided styles and meanings, and a '_____' which actively sought a minority style ...

 a. 28-hour day
 b. 33 Strategies of War
 c. Subculture
 d. 1990 Clean Air Act

Chapter 10. Organizational Culture

4. _____ is one of the managerial functions like planning, organizing, staffing and directing. It is an important function because it helps to check the errors and to take the corrective action so that deviation from standards are minimized and stated goals of the organization are achieved in desired manner. According to modern concepts, _____ is a foreseeing action whereas earlier concept of _____ was used only when errors were detected. _____ in management means setting standards, measuring actual performance and taking corrective action.
   a. Decision tree pruning
   b. Turnover
   c. Schedule of reinforcement
   d. Control

5. A _____ is a list of the general tasks and responsibilities of a position. Typically, it also includes to whom the position reports, specifications such as the qualifications needed by the person in the job, salary range for the position, etc. A _____ is usually developed by conducting a job analysis, which includes examining the tasks and sequences of tasks necessary to perform the job.
   a. Recruitment
   b. Recruitment advertising
   c. Recruitment Process Insourcing
   d. Job description

6. _____ is a form of applied ethics that examines ethical principles and moral or ethical problems that arise in a business environment. It applies to all aspects of business conduct and is relevant to the conduct of individuals and business organizations as a whole. Applied ethics is a field of ethics that deals with ethical questions in many fields such as medical, technical, legal and _____.
   a. Hypernorms
   b. Corporate Sustainability
   c. Business ethics
   d. Facilitation payments

7. In neuroscience, the _____ is a collection of brain structures which attempts to regulate and control behavior by inducing pleasurable effects.

A psychological reward is a process that reinforces behavior -- something that, when offered, causes a behavior to increase in intensity. Reward is an operational concept for describing the positive value an individual ascribes to an object, behavioral act or an internal physical state.

a. 33 Strategies of War
b. 28-hour day
c. 1990 Clean Air Act
d. Reward system

8. _____ refers to the stock of skills and knowledge embodied in the ability to perform labor so as to produce economic value. It is the skills and knowledge gained by a worker through education and experience. Many early economic theories refer to it simply as labor, one of three factors of production, and consider it to be a fungible resource -- homogeneous and easily interchangeable.
    a. Deflation
    b. Human capital
    c. Market structure
    d. Productivity management

9. _____ describes how content an individual is with his or her job.

The happier people are within their job, the more satisfied they are said to be. _____ is not the same as motivation, although it is clearly linked.

    a. Goal-setting theory
    b. Human relations
    c. Job satisfaction
    d. Job analysis

Chapter 11. Developing High-Performance Teams

1. _____ has been described as the 'process of social influence in which one person can enlist the aid and support of others in the accomplishment of a common task' . A definition more inclusive of followers comes from Alan Keith of Genentech who said '_____ is ultimately about creating a way for people to contribute to making something extraordinary happen.'

   _____ is one of the most salient aspects of the organizational context. However, defining _____ has been challenging.

   a. 1990 Clean Air Act
   b. Situational leadership
   c. 28-hour day
   d. Leadership

2. _____ refers to metrics and measures of output from production processes, per unit of input. Labor _____, for example, is typically measured as a ratio of output per labor-hour, an input. _____ may be conceived of as a metrics of the technical or engineering efficiency of production.
   a. Productivity
   b. Value engineering
   c. Master production schedule
   d. Remanufacturing

3. _____ is an advertisement in which a particular product specifically mentions a competitor by name for the express purpose of showing why the competitor is inferior to the product naming it.

   This should not be confused with parody advertisements, where a fictional product is being advertised for the purpose of poking fun at the particular advertisement, nor should it be confused with the use of a coined brand name for the purpose of comparing the product without actually naming an actual competitor. ('Wikipedia tastes better and is less filling than the Encyclopedia Galactica.')

   In the 1980s, during what has been referred to as the cola wars, soft-drink manufacturer Pepsi ran a series of advertisements where people, caught on hidden camera, in a blind taste test, chose Pepsi over rival Coca-Cola.

   a. Comparative advertising
   b. 33 Strategies of War
   c. 28-hour day
   d. 1990 Clean Air Act

Chapter 11. Developing High-Performance Teams

4. In the social psychology of groups, _____ is the phenomenon of people making less effort to achieve a goal when they work in a group than when they work alone. This is seen as one of the main reasons groups are sometimes less productive than the combined performance of their members working as individuals.

- Ringelmann, Max : 1913

Research began in 1913 with Max Ringelmann's study. He found that when he asked a group of men to pull on a rope, that they did not pull as hard, or put as much effort into the activity, as they did when they were pulling alone.

a. Personal space
b. Self-enhancement
c. Machiavellianism
d. Social loafing

5. A _____ -- also known as a geographically dispersed team -- is a group of individuals who work across time, space, and organizational boundaries with links strengthened by webs of communication technology. They have complementary skills and are committed to a common purpose, have interdependent performance goals, and share an approach to work for which they hold themselves mutually accountable. Geographically dispersed teams allow organizations to hire and retain the best people regardless of location.

a. Risk management
b. Trademark
c. Kanban
d. Virtual team

6. _____ is a dynamic of being mutually and physically responsible to and sharing a common set of principles with others. This concept differs distinctly from 'dependence' in that an interdependent relationship implies that all participants are emotionally, economically, ecologically and or morally 'interdependent.' Some people advocate freedom or independence as a sort of ultimate good; others do the same with devotion to one's family, community, or society. _____ recognizes the truth in each position and weaves them together.

a. A Stake in the Outcome
b. Interdependence
c. AAAI
d. A4e

7. _____ refers to the long-term management of intractable conflicts. It is the label for the variety of ways by which people handle grievances--standing up for what they consider to be right and against what they consider to be wrong. Those ways include such diverse phenomena as gossip, ridicule, lynching, terrorism, warfare, feuding, genocide, law, mediation, and avoidance.

Chapter 11. Developing High-Performance Teams

a. 1990 Clean Air Act
b. Conflict management
c. 33 Strategies of War
d. 28-hour day

8. Various _____ can be employed dependent on the culture of the business, the nature of the task, the nature of the workforce and the personality and skills of the leaders. This idea was further developed by Robert Tannenbaum and Warren H. Schmidt (1958, 1973) who argued that the style of leadership is dependent upon the prevailing circumstance; therefore leaders should exercise a range of leadership styles and should deploy them as appropriate.

An Autocratic or authoritarian manager makes all the decisions, keeping the information and decision making among the senior management.

a. 28-hour day
b. 1990 Clean Air Act
c. 33 Strategies of War
d. Management styles

9. _____, in psychology, are goals that are achieved by the contribution and co-operation of two or more people, with individual goals that are normally in opposition to each other, working together.

Muzafer Sherif (1954) performed a study involving a group of boys at a camp that were in opposition to one another, one named Eagles, one named the Rattlers, in a zero-sum situation. The opposing groups had strong negative feelings towards each other, resulting in hostile actions such as 'garbage wars'.

a. 1990 Clean Air Act
b. Superordinate goals
c. 28-hour day
d. 33 Strategies of War

Chapter 12. Staffing and Developing a Diverse Workforce

1. _____ is an increasingly broadening term with which an organization, or other human system describes the combination of traditionally administrative personnel functions with acquisition and application of skills, knowledge and experience, Employee Relations and resource planning at various levels. The field draws upon concepts developed in Industrial/Organizational Psychology and System Theory. _____ has at least two related interpretations depending on context. The original usage derives from political economy and economics, where it was traditionally called labor, one of four factors of production although this perspective is changing as a function of new and ongoing research into more strategic approaches at national levels. This first usage is used more in terms of '_____ development', and can go beyond just organizations to the level of nations. The more traditional usage within corporations and businesses refers to the individuals within a firm or agency, and to the portion of the organization that deals with hiring, firing, training, and other personnel issues, typically referred to as '_____ management'.

   a. Progressive discipline
   b. Human resource management
   c. Bradford Factor
   d. Human resources

2. In economics, _____ is the desire to own something and the ability to pay for it. The term _____ signifies the ability or the willingness to buy a particular commodity at a given point of time.

   a. 1990 Clean Air Act
   b. 28-hour day
   c. 33 Strategies of War
   d. Demand

3. _____ refers to various methodologies for analyzing the requirements of a job.

   The general purpose of _____ is to document the requirements of a job and the work performed. Job and task analysis is performed as a basis for later improvements, including: definition of a job domain; describing a job; developing performance appraisals, selection systems, promotion criteria, training needs assessment, and compensation plans.

   a. Hersey-Blanchard situational theory
   b. Work design
   c. Management process
   d. Job analysis

Chapter 12. Staffing and Developing a Diverse Workforce

4. _____, also sometimes known as casual work, is a neologism which describes a type of employment relationship between an employer and employee. There is no universally agreed consensus on what type of working arrangement constitutes _____, but it is generally considered to be any one or combination of the following:

- Work which is temporary or lacks job security
- Work which is part time
- Work which is paid on a piece work basis

Whether a person who does _____ can be described as 'having a job' is debatable - however, _____ is usually not considered to be a career, or part of a career. One of the features of _____ is that it usually offers little or no opportunity for career development.

If a job is full time, permanent, and either pays a regular salary or a fixed wage for regular hours, then it is usually not considered to be _____.

a. 28-hour day
b. Contingent work
c. 1990 Clean Air Act
d. 33 Strategies of War

5. A _____ is a provisional group of workers who work for an organization on a non-permanent basis independent professionals, temporary contract workers, independent contractors or consultants. _____ Management is the strategic approach to managing an organization's _____ in a way that it reduces the company's cost in the management of contingent employees and mitigates the company's risk in employing them.

According to the US Bureau of Labor Statistics, the nontraditional workforce includes 'multiple job holders, contingent and part-time workers, and people in alternative work arrangements.' These workers currently represent a substantial portion of the U.S. workforce, and 'nearly four out of five employers, in establishments of all sizes and industries, use some form of nontraditional staffing.' 'People in alternative work arrangements' includes independent contractors, employees of contract companies, workers who are on call, and temporary workers.

a. 33 Strategies of War
b. Contingent workforce
c. 1990 Clean Air Act
d. 28-hour day

6. The _____ is the labour pool in employment. It is generally used to describe those working for a single company or industry, but can also apply to a geographic region like a city, country, state, etc. The term generally excludes the employers or management, and implies those involved in manual labour.

a. Pink-collar worker
b. Work-life balance
c. Division of labour
d. Workforce

7. Organizational culture is not the same as _____. It is wider and deeper concepts, something that an organization 'is' rather than what it 'has' (according to Buchanan and Huczynski.)

_____ is the total sum of the values, customs, traditions and meanings that make a company unique.

a. Corporate culture
b. Path-goal theory
c. Work design
d. Job analysis

8. The 'business case for _____', theorizes that in a global marketplace, a company that employs a diverse workforce (both men and women, people of many generations, people from ethnically and racially diverse backgrounds etc.) is better able to understand the demographics of the marketplace it serves and is thus better equipped to thrive in that marketplace than a company that has a more limited range of employee demographics.

An additional corollary suggests that a company that supports the _____ of its workforce can also improve employee satisfaction, productivity and retention.

a. Trademark
b. Kanban
c. Virtual team
d. Diversity

9. A _____ is a list of the general tasks and responsibilities of a position. Typically, it also includes to whom the position reports, specifications such as the qualifications needed by the person in the job, salary range for the position, etc. A _____ is usually developed by conducting a job analysis, which includes examining the tasks and sequences of tasks necessary to perform the job.

a. Recruitment advertising
b. Recruitment
c. Job description
d. Recruitment Process Insourcing

Chapter 12. Staffing and Developing a Diverse Workforce

10. _____, commonly abbreviated to Gen X, is a term used to refer to a generational cohort of children born after the baby boom ended and usually prior to the 1980s

The term _____ has been used in demography, the social sciences, and marketing, though it is most often used in popular culture.

In the U.S. _____ was originally referred to as the 'baby bust' generation because of the drop in the birth rate following the baby boom.

  a. Adam Smith
  b. Generation X
  c. Affiliation
  d. Abraham Harold Maslow

11. _____ is a term used to describe the demographic cohort following Generation X. Its members are often referred to as 'Millennials' or 'Echo Boomers') . There are no precise dates for when Gen Y begins and ends. Most commentators use dates from the early 1980s to early 1990s.
  a. Giovanni Agnelli
  b. David Wittig
  c. Benjamin R. Barber
  d. Generation Y

12. The _____ of 1967, Pub. L. No. 90-202, 81 Stat. 602 (Dec. 15, 1967), codified as Chapter 14 of Title 29 of the United States Code, 29 U.S.C. § 621 through 29 U.S.C. § 634 (ADEA), prohibits employment discrimination against persons 40 years of age or older in the United States). The law also sets standards for pensions and benefits provided by employers and requires that information about the needs of older workers be provided to the general public.
  a. Extra time
  b. Age Discrimination in Employment Act
  c. Unemployment and Farm Relief Act
  d. Undue hardship

13. The _____ of 1990 (ADA) is the short title of United States (Pub.L. 101-336, 104 Stat. 327, enacted July 26, 1990), codified at 42 U.S.C. § 12101 et seq. It was signed into law on July 26, 1990, by President George H. W. Bush, and later amended with changes effective January 1, 2009. The ADA is a wide-ranging civil rights law that prohibits, under certain circumstances, discrimination based on disability. It affords similar protections against discrimination to Americans with disabilities as the Civil Rights Act of 1964,

Chapter 12. Staffing and Developing a Diverse Workforce

   a. Employment discrimination
   b. Australian labour law
   c. Equal Pay Act of 1963
   d. Americans with Disabilities Act

14.   In employment law, a (BFOQ) (US) or bona fide occupational requirement (BFOR) (Canada) is a quality or an attribute that employers are allowed to consider when making decisions on the hiring and retention of employees - qualities that, when considered, in other contexts would be considered discriminatory and thus violating civil rights employment law.

In employment discrimination law in the United States, United States Code Title 29 , Chapter 14 (age discrimination in employment), section 623 (prohibition of age discrimination) establishes that 'It shall not be unlawful for an employer, employment agency, or labor organization (1) to take any action otherwise prohibited under subsections (a), (b), (c), or (e) of this section where age is a _____ reasonably necessary to the normal operation of the particular business, or where the differentiation is based on reasonable factors other than age, or where such practices involve an employee in a workplace in a foreign country, and compliance with such subsections would cause such employer, or a corporation controlled by such employer, to violate the laws of the country in which such workplace is located.'

One example of _____s are mandatory retirement ages for bus drivers and airline pilots, for safety reasons. Further, in advertising, a manufacturer of men's clothing may lawfully advertise for male models.

   a. MacPherson v. Buick Motor Co.
   b. Sick leave
   c. Corporate governance
   d. Bona fide occupational qualification

15.   The _____ was a landmark piece of legislation in the United States that outlawed racial segregation in schools, public places, and employment.
   a. Civil Rights Act of 1964
   b. Negligence in employment
   c. Design patent
   d. Financial Security Law of France

16.   The _____ is a United States statute that was passed in response to a series of United States Supreme Court decisions which limited the rights of employees who had sued their employers for discrimination. The Act represented the first effort since the passage of the Civil Rights Act of 1964 to modify some of the basic procedural and substantive rights provided by federal law in employment discrimination cases. It provided for the right to trial by jury on discrimination claims and introduced the possibility of emotional distress damages, while limiting the amount that a jury could award

Chapter 12. Staffing and Developing a Diverse Workforce

The 1991 Act combined elements from two different civil rights acts of the past: the Civil Rights Act of 1866, better known by the number assigned to it in the codification of federal laws as 'Section 1981', and the employment-related provisions of the Civil Rights Act of 1964, generally referred to as 'Title VII', its location within the Act.

   a. Civil Rights Act of 1991
   b. Covenant
   c. Resource Conservation and Recovery Act
   d. Negligence in employment

17. _____ is a contract between two parties, one being the employer and the other being the employee. An employee may be defined as: 'A person in the service of another under any contract of hire, express or implied, oral or written, where the employer has the power or right to control and direct the employee in the material details of how the work is to be performed.' Black's Law Dictionary page 471 (5th ed. 1979.)

   a. Employment counsellor
   b. Exit interview
   c. Employment
   d. Employment rate

18. _____ refers to discriminatory employment practices such as bias in hiring, promotion, job assignment, termination, and compensation, and various types of harassment.

In many countries, laws prohibit employers from discriminating on the basis of race, color, sex, religion, national origin, physical or mental disability, or age. There is also a growing body of law preventing or occasionally justifying _____ based on sexual orientation or gender identity.

   a. Invitee
   b. Extra time
   c. Employee Retirement Income Security Act
   d. Employment discrimination

19. The _____ 1970 is an Act of the United Kingdom Parliament which prohibits any less favourable treatment between men and women in terms of pay and conditions of employment. It came into force on 29 December 1975. The term pay is interpreted in a broad sense to include, on top of wages, things like holidays, pension rights, company perks and some kinds of bonuses.

Chapter 12. Staffing and Developing a Diverse Workforce

   a. Architectural Barriers Act of 1968
   b. Australian labour law
   c. Oncale v. Sundowner Offshore Services
   d. Equal Pay Act

20. The _____, Pub. L. No. 88-38, 77 Stat. 56, (June 10, 1963) codified at 29 U.S.C. § 206(d), is a United States federal law amending the Fair Labor Standards Act, aimed at abolishing wage differentials based on sex. In passing the bill, Congress denounces sex discrimination.
   a. Invitee
   b. Architectural Barriers Act of 1968
   c. Equal Pay Act of 1963
   d. Extra time

21. The _____ is a United States labor law allowing an employee to take unpaid leave due to a serious health condition that makes the employee unable to perform his job or to care for a sick family member or to care for a new son or daughter (including by birth, adoption or foster care.) The bill was among the first signed into law by President Bill Clinton in his first term.
   a. Family and Medical Leave Act of 1993
   b. Sarbanes-Oxley Act of 2002
   c. Contributory negligence
   d. Harvester Judgment

22. The U.S. _____ of 1973 prohibits discrimination on the basis of disability in programs conducted by Federal agencies, in programs receiving Federal financial assistance, in Federal employment, and in the employment practices of Federal contractors. The standards for determining employment discrimination under the _____ are the same as those used in title I of the Americans with Disabilities Act.

There are four key sections of the Act.

   a. 1990 Clean Air Act
   b. Rehabilitation Act
   c. 33 Strategies of War
   d. 28-hour day

23. _____ refers to the process of screening, and selecting qualified people for a job at an organization or firm mid- and large-size organizations and companies often retain professional recruiters or outsource some of the process to _____ agencies. External _____ is the process of attracting and selecting employees from outside the organization.

Chapter 12. Staffing and Developing a Diverse Workforce

The _____ industry has four main types of agencies: employment agencies, _____ websites and job search engines, 'headhunters' for executive and professional _____, and in-house _____.

a. Labour hire
b. Recruitment Process Outsourcing
c. Referral recruitment
d. Recruitment

24. A _____ is a name or trademark connected with a product or producer. _____s have become increasingly important components of culture and the economy, now being described as 'cultural accessories and personal philosophies'.

Some people distinguish the psychological aspect of a _____ from the experiential aspect.

a. Brand awareness
b. Brand extension
c. Brand loyalty
d. Brand

25. The term _____ in logic applies to arguments or statements.

An argument is valid if and only if the truth of its premises entails the truth of its conclusion, it would be self-contradictory to affirm the premises and deny the conclusion. The corresponding conditional of a valid argument is a logical truth and the negation of its corresponding conditional is a contradiction.

a. 1990 Clean Air Act
b. Simplification
c. Fuzzy logic
d. Validity

26. In US employment law, _____ is defined as a substantially different rate of selection in hiring, promotion sex statistical significance tests, and/or practical significance tests. _____ is often used interchangeably with 'disparate impact,' which was a legal term coined in one of the most significant U.S. Supreme Court rulings on disparate or _____: Griggs v. Duke Power Co., 1971.

a. AAAI
b. A Stake in the Outcome
c. A4e
d. Adverse impact

27.

The terms _____ and positive action refer to policies that take race, ethnicity, or gender into consideration in an attempt to promote equal opportunity. The focus of such policies ranges from employment and education to public contracting and health programs. The impetus towards _____ is twofold: to maximize diversity in all levels of society, along with its presumed benefits, and to redress perceived disadvantages due to overt, institutional, or involuntary discrimination.

a. Affirmative action
b. Adam Smith
c. Affiliation
d. Abraham Harold Maslow

28. In business and economics, _____ is a business resource assessment tool enabling a company to compare its actual performance with its potential performance. At its core are two questions: 'Where are we?' and 'Where do we want to be?' If a company or organization is under-utilizing its current resources or is forgoing investment in capital or technology, then it may be producing or performing at a level below its potential. This concept is similar to the base case of being below one's production possibilities frontier.
a. Business networking
b. Cross-selling
c. Yield management
d. Gap analysis

29. _____ is an educational process whereby the participant studies their own actions and experience in order to improve performance. This concept is close to learning-by-doing and teaching through examples and repetitions.

_____ is done in conjunction with others, in small groups called _____ sets or two-in, two-out team.

a. A Stake in the Outcome
b. Action learning
c. AAAI
d. A4e

Chapter 12. Staffing and Developing a Diverse Workforce

30. _____ is an approach to management development where an individual is moved through a schedule of assignments designed to give him or her a breadth of exposure to the entire operation.

_____ is also practiced to allow qualified employees to gain more insights into the processes of a company, and to reduce boredom and increase job satisfaction through job variation.

The term _____ can also mean the scheduled exchange of persons in offices, especially in public offices, prior to the end of incumbency or the legislative period.

a. 28-hour day
b. 1990 Clean Air Act
c. 33 Strategies of War
d. Job rotation

31. There are two types of _____ relationships: formal and informal. Informal relationships develop on their own between partners. Formal _____, on the other hand, refers to assigned relationships, often associated with organizational _____ programs designed to promote employee development or to assist at-risk children and youth.
a. Real Property Administrator
b. Fix it twice
c. Mentoring
d. Human resource management system

Chapter 13. Motivating and Rewarding Employee Performance

1. _____, also erroneously called Work engagement, is a widely employed, yet poorly defined concept, developed principally from the consulting community. As a result, each consulting firm asserts different definitions of the concept, component elements (commitment, job satisfaction, pride, job commitment, discretionary effort. etc), and resulting business outcomes.
   a. A Stake in the Outcome
   b. AAAI
   c. Employee engagement
   d. A4e

2. _____ of individual behavior or MARS BAR model of individual behavior or simply _____ is a model that seeks to explain individual behavior as a result of internal and external factors or influences acting together . The name of the model is an acronym for individual Motivation, Abilities, Role Perception and Situational Factors. These are seen as the four major factors in determining individual behavior and results.
   a. Teasing
   b. 1990 Clean Air Act
   c. 28-hour day
   d. MARS model

3. _____ is a term that has been used in various psychology theories, often in slightly different ways (e.g., Goldstein, Maslow, Rogers.) The term was originally introduced by the organismic theorist Kurt Goldstein for the motive to realise all of one's potentialities. In his view, it is the master motive--indeed, the only real motive a person has, all others being merely manifestations of it.
   a. 33 Strategies of War
   b. 28-hour day
   c. 1990 Clean Air Act
   d. Self-actualization

4. In law, _____ is the term to describe a partnership between two or more parties.

In England a number of statutes on the subject have been passed, the chief being the Bastardy Act of 1845, and the Bastardy Laws Amendment Acts of 1872 and 1873. The mother of a bastard may summon the putative father to petty sessions within twelve months of the birth (or at any later time if he is proved to have contributed to the child's support within twelve months after the birth), and the justices, as after hearing evidence on both sides, may, if the mother's evidence be corroborated in some material particular, adjudge the man to be the putative father of the child, and order him to pay a sum not exceeding five shillings a week for its maintenance, together with a sum for expenses incidental to the birth, or the funeral expenses, if it has died before the date of order, and the costs of the proceedings.

a. Affiliation
b. Affirmative action
c. Abraham Harold Maslow
d. Adam Smith

5. _____ refers to an individual's desire for significant accomplishment, mastering of skills, control, or high standards. The term was introduced by the psychologist, David McClelland.

_____ is related to the difficulty of tasks people choose to undertake.

a. Two-factor theory
b. 1990 Clean Air Act
c. Need for power
d. Need for achievement

6. The _____ is a term that was popularised by David McClelland and describes a person's need to feel a sense of involvement and 'belonging' within a social group. However, it should be recognised that McClellend's thinking was strongly influenced by the pioneering work of Henry Murray who first identified underlying psychological human needs and motivational processes (1938.) It was Murray who set out a taxonomy of needs, including Achievement, Power and Affiliation - and placed these in the context of an integrated motivational model.
a. SESAMO
b. Strong-Campbell Interest Inventory
c. Polynomial conjoint measurement
d. Need for affiliation

7. _____ is a term that was popularized by renowned psychologist David McClelland in 1961. However, it should be recognized that McClellend's thinking was strongly influenced by the pioneering work of Henry Murray who first identified underlying psychological human needs and motivational processes (1938.) It was Murray who set out a taxonomy of needs, including Achievement, Power and Affiliation - and placed these in the context of an integrated motivational model.
a. Two-factor theory
b. 1990 Clean Air Act
c. Need for power
d. Need for Achievement

8. The phrase mergers and _____s refers to the aspect of corporate strategy, corporate finance and management dealing with the buying, selling and combining of different companies that can aid, finance, or help a growing company in a given industry grow rapidly without having to create another business entity.

An _____, also known as a takeover or a buyout, is the buying of one company (the 'target') by another. An _____ may be friendly or hostile.

 a. A4e
 b. A Stake in the Outcome
 c. AAAI
 d. Acquisition

9. _____ describes the situation when output from (or information about the result of) an event or phenomenon in the past will influence the same event/phenomenon in the present or future. When an event is part of a chain of cause-and-effect that forms a circuit or loop, then the event is said to 'feed back' into itself.

_____ is also a synonym for:

- _____ signal; the information about the initial event that is the basis for subsequent modification of the event.
- _____ loop; the causal path that leads from the initial generation of the _____ signal to the subsequent modification of the event.

_____ is a mechanism, process or signal that is looped back to control a system within itself. Such a loop is called a _____ loop.

 a. Feedback loop
 b. 1990 Clean Air Act
 c. Positive feedback
 d. Feedback

10. _____ involves establishing specific, measurable and time-targeted objectives. Work on the theory of goal-setting suggests that it's an effective tool for making progress by ensuring that participants in a group with a common goal are clearly aware of what is expected from them if an objective is to be achieved. On a personal level, setting goals is a process that allows people to specify then work towards their own objectives - most commonly with financial or career-based goals.
 a. Digital strategy
 b. Goal setting
 c. Resource-based view
 d. Catfish effect

Chapter 13. Motivating and Rewarding Employee Performance

11. _____ is about the mental processes regarding choice, or choosing. It explains the processes that an individual undergoes to make choices. In organizational behavior study, _____ is a motivation theory first proposed by Victor Vroom of the Yale School of Management.

   a. AAAI
   b. Expectancy theory
   c. A Stake in the Outcome
   d. A4e

12. In game theory, an _____ is a set of moves or strategies taken by the players, or their payoffs resulting from the actions or strategies taken by all players. The two are complementary in that given knowledge of the set of strategies of all players, the final state of the game is known, as are any relevant payoffs. In a game where chance or a random event is involved, the _____ is not known from only the set of strategies, but is only realized when the random event(s) are realized.

   a. A Stake in the Outcome
   b. A4e
   c. AAAI
   d. Outcome

13. _____ is the process of systematically determining a relative value of jobs in an organisation. In all cases the idea is to evaluate the job, not the person doing it.

   - Job Ranking is the most simple form. Basically you just order the jobs according to perceived seniority. It's easy in a small organization, but get exponentially difficult with lots of different jobs.

   - Pair Comparison introduces more rigour by comparing jobs in pairs, but really it's a more structured way of building a basic rank order.

   - Benchmarking or slotting sets up certain jobs that are analysed in detail. These are then used for comparison to slot jobs against these benchmarks.

   a. 1990 Clean Air Act
   b. 33 Strategies of War
   c. 28-hour day
   d. Job evaluation

14. Piece work or piecework describes types of employment in which a worker is paid a fixed '_____' for each unit produced or action performed. Piece work is also a form of performance-related pay (Piece rateP) and is the oldest form of performance pay.

Chapter 13. Motivating and Rewarding Employee Performance

In a manufacturing setting, the output of piece work can be measured by the number of physical items (pieces) produced, such as when a garment worker is paid per operational step completed, regardless of the time required.

a. Scientific management
b. Piecework
c. Piece rate
d. Methods-time measurement

15. The _____ is a performance management tool for measuring whether the smaller-scale operational activities of a company are aligned with its larger-scale objectives in terms of vision and strategy.

By focusing not only on financial outcomes but also on the operational, marketing and developmental inputs to these, the _____ helps provide a more comprehensive view of a business, which in turn helps organizations act in their best long-term interests. This tool is also being used to address business response to climate change and greenhouse gas emissions.

a. Commercial management
b. Balanced scorecard
c. Management development
d. Middle management

16. _____ is a method by which the job performance of an employee is evaluated _____ is a part of career development.

_____s are regular reviews of employee performance within organizations

Generally, the aims of a _____ are to:

- Give feedback on performance to employees.
- Identify employee training needs.
- Document criteria used to allocate organizational rewards.
- Form a basis for personnel decisions: salary increases, promotions, disciplinary actions, etc.
- Provide the opportunity for organizational diagnosis and development.
- Facilitate communication between employee and administraton
- Validate selection techniques and human resource policies to meet federal Equal Employment Opportunity requirements.

Chapter 13. Motivating and Rewarding Employee Performance

A common approach to assessing performance is to use a numerical or scalar rating system whereby managers are asked to score an individual against a number of objectives/attributes. In some companies, employees receive assessments from their manager, peers, subordinates and customers while also performing a self assessment.

a. Personnel management
b. Progressive discipline
c. Performance appraisal
d. Human resource management

17. In finance, an _____ is a contract between a buyer and a seller that gives the buyer the right--but not the obligation-- to buy or to sell a particular asset (the underlying asset) at a later day at an agreed price. In return for granting the _____, the seller collects a payment (the premium) from the buyer. A call _____ gives the buyer the right to buy the underlying asset; a put _____ gives the buyer of the _____ the right to sell the underlying asset.

a. A Stake in the Outcome
b. AAAI
c. A4e
d. Option

18. _____ is the state or fact of exclusive rights and control over property, which may be an object, land/real estate or intellectual property. An _____ right is also referred to as title. The concept of _____ has existed for thousands of years and in all cultures.

a. A Stake in the Outcome
b. A4e
c. Emanation of the state
d. Ownership

19. In human resources or industrial/organizational psychology, _____ ' 'multisource feedback,' or 'multisource assessment,' is feedback that comes from all around an employee. '360' refers to the 360 degrees in a circle, with an individual figuratively in the center of the circle. Feedback is provided by subordinates, peers, and supervisors.

a. Job knowledge
b. 360-degree feedback
c. Personnel management
d. Revolving door syndrome

20. _____ attempts to explain relational satisfaction in terms of perceptions of fair/unfair distributions of resources within interpersonal relationships. _____ is considered as one of the justice theories, It was first developed in 1962 by John Stacey Adams, a workplace and behavioral psychologist, who asserted that employees seek to maintain equity between the inputs that they bring to a job and the outcomes that they receive from it against the perceived inputs and outcomes of others (Adams, 1965.) The belief is that people value fair treatment which causes them to be motivated to keep the fairness maintained within the relationships of their co-workers and the organization.

   a. AAAI
   b. A4e
   c. Equity theory
   d. A Stake in the Outcome

21. _____ refers to the stock of skills and knowledge embodied in the ability to perform labor so as to produce economic value. It is the skills and knowledge gained by a worker through education and experience. Many early economic theories refer to it simply as labor, one of three factors of production, and consider it to be a fungible resource -- homogeneous and easily interchangeable.

   a. Productivity management
   b. Market structure
   c. Deflation
   d. Human capital

22. _____ refers to increasing the spiritual, political, social or economic strength of individuals and communities. It often involves the empowered developing confidence in their own capacities.

The term Human _____ covers a vast landscape of meanings, interpretations, definitions and disciplines ranging from psychology and philosophy to the highly commercialized Self-Help industry and Motivational sciences.

   a. A Stake in the Outcome
   b. AAAI
   c. A4e
   d. Empowerment

23. _____ is an attempt to motivate employees by giving them the opportunity to use the range of their abilities. It is an idea that was developed by the American psychologist Frederick Herzberg in the 1950s. It can be contrasted to job enlargement which simply increases the number of tasks without changing the challenge.

a. Cash cow
b. Catfish effect
c. C-A-K-E
d. Job enrichment

Chapter 14. Managing Employee Attitudes and Well-Being

1. _____ is an uncomfortable feeling caused by holding two contradictory ideas simultaneously. The 'ideas' or 'cognitions' in question may include attitudes and beliefs, and also the awareness of one's behavior. The theory of _____ proposes that people have a motivational drive to reduce dissonance by changing their attitudes, beliefs, and behaviors, or by justifying or rationalizing their attitudes, beliefs, and behaviors.

   a. Trait theory
   b. Quantitative psychology
   c. Cognitive bias
   d. Cognitive dissonance

2. _____ describes how content an individual is with his or her job.

   The happier people are within their job, the more satisfied they are said to be. _____ is not the same as motivation, although it is clearly linked.

   a. Human relations
   b. Goal-setting theory
   c. Job analysis
   d. Job satisfaction

3. _____, a business term, is a measure of how products and services supplied by a company meet or surpass customer expectation. It is seen as a key performance indicator within business and is part of the four perspectives of a Balanced Scorecard.

   In a competitive marketplace where businesses compete for customers, _____ is seen as a key differentiator and increasingly has become a key element of business strategy.

   a. Critical Success Factor
   b. Horizontal integration
   c. Foreign ownership
   d. Customer satisfaction

4. A _____ exists when an employee experiences workplace harassment and fears going to work because of the offensive, intimidating religion, sex, national origin, age, disability, veteran status, or, in some jurisdictions, sexual orientation, political affiliation, citizenship status, marital status, or personal appearance. _____ is also one of the two legal categories of sexual harassment.

   The anti-discrimination statutes governing _____ are not a general civility code.

Chapter 14. Managing Employee Attitudes and Well-Being

a. Contrat nouvelle embauche
b. Flextime
c. Financial Security Law of France
d. Hostile work environment

5. _____, which can be translated literally from Japanese as 'death from overwork', is occupational sudden death. Although this category has a significant count, Japan is one of the few countries that reports it in the statistics as a separate category. The major medical causes of _____ deaths are heart attack and stroke due to stress.
   a. 1990 Clean Air Act
   b. Karoshi
   c. 33 Strategies of War
   d. 28-hour day

6. _____ indicates a more-or-less equal exchange or substitution of goods or services. English speakers often use the term to mean 'a favour for a favour' and the phrases with almost identical meaning include: 'what for what,' 'give and take,' 'tit for tat', 'this for that', and 'you scratch my back, and I'll scratch yours'.

In legal usage, _____ indicates that an item or a service has been traded in return for something of value, usually when the propriety or equity of the transaction is in question.

   a. Quid pro quo
   b. 1990 Clean Air Act
   c. 28-hour day
   d. 33 Strategies of War

7. _____ is unwelcome harassment of a sexual nature, or based upon the receiving party's sex or gender. In some contexts or circumstances, _____ may be illegal. It includes a range of behavior from seemingly mild transgressions and annoyances to actual sexual abuse or sexual assault.
   a. 28-hour day
   b. 1990 Clean Air Act
   c. Hypernorms
   d. Sexual harassment

8. _____ is one of the managerial functions like planning, organizing, staffing and directing. It is an important function because it helps to check the errors and to take the corrective action so that deviation from standards are minimized and stated goals of the organization are achieved in desired manner. According to modern concepts, _____ is a foreseeing action whereas earlier concept of _____ was used only when errors were detected. _____ in management means setting standards, measuring actual performance and taking corrective action.

a. Turnover
b. Control
c. Schedule of reinforcement
d. Decision tree pruning

9. _____ refers to the stock of skills and knowledge embodied in the ability to perform labor so as to produce economic value. It is the skills and knowledge gained by a worker through education and experience. Many early economic theories refer to it simply as labor, one of three factors of production, and consider it to be a fungible resource -- homogeneous and easily interchangeable.
   a. Productivity management
   b. Market structure
   c. Deflation
   d. Human capital

10. _____ is a broad concept including proper prioritizing between career and ambition on one hand, compared with pleasure, leisure, family and spiritual development on the other.

As the separation between work and home life has diminished, this concept has become more relevant than ever before.

The expression was first used in the late 1970s to describe the balance between an individual's work and personal life.

   a. Workforce
   b. Work-life balance
   c. Quality of working life
   d. Division of labour

11. The _____ is a United States labor law allowing an employee to take unpaid leave due to a serious health condition that makes the employee unable to perform his job or to care for a sick family member or to care for a new son or daughter (including by birth, adoption or foster care.) The bill was among the first signed into law by President Bill Clinton in his first term.
   a. Family and Medical Leave Act of 1993
   b. Contributory negligence
   c. Harvester Judgment
   d. Sarbanes-Oxley Act of 2002

Chapter 14. Managing Employee Attitudes and Well-Being

12. _____, e-commuting, e-work, telework, working from home (WFH), or working at home (WAH) is a work arrangement in which employees enjoy flexibility in working location and hours. In other words, the daily commute to a central place of work is replaced by telecommunication links. Many work from home, while others, occasionally also referred to as nomad workers or web commuters utilize mobile telecommunications technology to work from coffee shops or myriad other locations.
   a. 1990 Clean Air Act
   b. Telecommuting
   c. 33 Strategies of War
   d. 28-hour day

13. The trait of _____ is a central dimension of human personality. Extraverts (also spelled extroverts) tend to be gregarious, assertive, and interested in seeking out excitement. Introverts, in contrast, tend to be more reserved, less outgoing, and less sociable.
   a. A4e
   b. Extraversion-introversion
   c. A Stake in the Outcome
   d. AAAI

14. _____ is one of five major domains of personality discovered by psychologists. Openness involves active imagination, aesthetic sensitivity, attentiveness to inner feelings, preference for variety, and intellectual curiosity. A great deal of psychometric research has demonstrated that these qualities are statistically correlated.
   a. Openness to experience
   b. Extraversion
   c. Introversion
   d. Introverts

15. _____ is a term defined by the Oxford English Dictionary as an individual's 'course or progress through life '. It is usually considered to pertain to remunerative work (and sometimes also formal education.)

The etymology of the term is somewhat ironic in that it comes from the Latin word carrera, which means race .

   a. Spatial mismatch
   b. Nursing shortage
   c. Career
   d. Career planning

Chapter 15. Managing through Power, Influence, and Negotiation

1. _____ is the theory of political modification of markets, formulated by American economist John Kenneth Galbraith in his 1952 book American Capitalism.

In the classic liberal economy, goods and services are provided and prices set by free bargaining.

Modern economies give massive powers to large business corporations to bias this process, and there arise 'countervailing' powers in the form of trade unions, citizens' organizations and so on, to offset business's excessive advantage.

   a. 33 Strategies of War
   b. Countervailing power
   c. 1990 Clean Air Act
   d. 28-hour day

2. _____ is one of the managerial functions like planning, organizing, staffing and directing. It is an important function because it helps to check the errors and to take the corrective action so that deviation from standards are minimized and stated goals of the organization are achieved in desired manner. According to modern concepts, _____ is a foreseeing action whereas earlier concept of _____ was used only when errors were detected. _____ in management means setting standards, measuring actual performance and taking corrective action.

   a. Turnover
   b. Schedule of reinforcement
   c. Decision tree pruning
   d. Control

3. Within graph theory and network analysis, there are various measures of the _____ of a vertex within a graph that determine the relative importance of a vertex within the graph (for example, how important a person is within a social network, or, in the theory of space syntax, how important a room is within a building or how well-used a road is within an urban network.)

There are four measures of _____ that are widely used in network analysis: degree _____, betweenness, closeness, and eigenvector _____.

The first, and simplest, is degree _____.

   a. 28-hour day
   b. 33 Strategies of War
   c. 1990 Clean Air Act
   d. Centrality

4. The _____ is a leadership theory in the field of organizational studies developed by Robert House in 1971 and revised in 1996. The theory that a leader's behavior is contingent to the satisfaction, motivation and performance of subordinates. The revised version also argues that the leader engage in behaviors that complement subordinate's abilities and compensate for deficiencies.
   a. Sociotechnical systems
   b. Path-goal theory
   c. Corporate Culture
   d. Human relations

5. _____ is a trait taught by many personal development experts and psychotherapists and the subject of many popular self-help books. It is linked to self-esteem and considered an important communication skill.

As a communication style and strategy, _____ is distinguished from aggression and passivity.

   a. Intrinsic motivation
   b. A Stake in the Outcome
   c. A4e
   d. Assertiveness

6. A _____ is an alliance among individuals or groups, during which they cooperate in joint action, each in his own self-interest, joining forces together for a common cause. This alliance may be temporary or a matter of convenience. A _____ thus differs from a more formal covenant.
   a. Coalition
   b. 33 Strategies of War
   c. 1990 Clean Air Act
   d. 28-hour day

7. In sociology and social psychology, _____ is the process through which people try to control the impressions other people form of them. It is a goal-directed conscious or unconscious attempt to influence the perceptions of other people about a person, object or event by regulating and controlling information in social interaction. It is usually used synonymously with self-presentation, if a person tries to influence the perception of their image.
   a. A Stake in the Outcome
   b. A4e
   c. AAAI
   d. Impression management

8. _____ is a form of social influence. It is the process of guiding people and oneself toward the adoption of an idea, attitude, or action by rational and symbolic (though not always logical) means. It is strategy of problem-solving relying on 'appeals' rather than coercion.
   a. Social loafing
   b. Self-enhancement
   c. Personal space
   d. Persuasion

9. _____ of individual behavior or MARS BAR model of individual behavior or simply _____ is a model that seeks to explain individual behavior as a result of internal and external factors or influences acting together. The name of the model is an acronym for individual Motivation, Abilities, Role Perception and Situational Factors. These are seen as the four major factors in determining individual behavior and results.
   a. Teasing
   b. 28-hour day
   c. MARS model
   d. 1990 Clean Air Act

Chapter 16. Effective Leadership

83

1. _____ has been described as the 'process of social influence in which one person can enlist the aid and support of others in the accomplishment of a common task' . A definition more inclusive of followers comes from Alan Keith of Genentech who said '_____ is ultimately about creating a way for people to contribute to making something extraordinary happen.'

_____ is one of the most salient aspects of the organizational context. However, defining _____ has been challenging.

   a. 1990 Clean Air Act
   b. 28-hour day
   c. Situational leadership
   d. Leadership

2. Recent strategic thought points ever more clearly towards the conclusion that the critical strategic question is not 'What?,' but 'Why?' The work of Mintzberg and others who draw a distinction between strategic planning (defined as systematic programming of pre-identified strategies) and _____ supports that conclusion. Intensified exploration of strategy from new directions is now coming together in the concept of what is being called _____. At this point, there is no generally accepted definition of the term, no common agreement as to its role or importance, and no standardized list of key competencies of strategic thinkers.
   a. Strategic drift
   b. Switching cost
   c. Complementors
   d. Strategic thinking

3. _____ of individual behavior or MARS BAR model of individual behavior or simply _____ is a model that seeks to explain individual behavior as a result of internal and external factors or influences acting together . The name of the model is an acronym for individual Motivation, Abilities, Role Perception and Situational Factors. These are seen as the four major factors in determining individual behavior and results.
   a. 1990 Clean Air Act
   b. MARS model
   c. Teasing
   d. 28-hour day

4. _____ , often measured as an _____ Quotient (EQ), is a term that describes the ability, capacity, skill or (in the case of the trait _____ model) a self-perceived ability, to identify, assess, and manage the emotions of one's self, of others, and of groups. Different models have been proposed for the definition of _____ and disagreement exists as to how the term should be used. Despite these disagreements, which are often highly technical, the ability _____ and trait _____ models (but not the mixed models) are enjoying considerable support in the literature and have successful applications in many different domains.

a. A4e
b. A Stake in the Outcome
c. Emotional intelligence
d. AAAI

5. _____ is a class of behavioural theory that claims that there is no best way to organize a corporation, to lead a company, or to make decisions. Instead, the optimal course of action is contingent (dependant) upon the internal and external situation. Several contingency approaches were developed concurrently in the late 1960s.
   a. Capability management
   b. Commercial management
   c. Distributed management
   d. Contingency theory

6. The _____ is a leadership theory in the field of organizational studies developed by Robert House in 1971 and revised in 1996. The theory that a leader's behavior is contingent to the satisfaction, motivation and performance of subordinates. The revised version also argues that the leader engage in behaviors that complement subordinate's abilities and compensate for deficiencies.
   a. Sociotechnical systems
   b. Corporate Culture
   c. Path-goal theory
   d. Human relations

7. _____ is a leadership style that defines as leadership that creates voluble and positive change in the followers. A transformational leader focuses on 'transforming' others to help each other, to look out for each other, be encouraging, harmonious, and look out for the organization as a whole. In this leadership, the leader enhances the motivation, moral and performance of his follower group.
   a. SESAMO
   b. Polynomial conjoint measurement
   c. Transformational leadership
   d. Strong-Campbell Interest Inventory

8. _____ is an idea in the field of Organizational studies and management which describes the psychology, attitudes, experiences, beliefs and Values (personal and cultural values) of an organization. It has been defined as 'the specific collection of values and norms that are shared by people and groups in an organization and that control the way they interact with each other and with stakeholders outside the organization.'

Chapter 16. Effective Leadership

This definition continues to explain organizational values also known as 'beliefs and ideas about what kinds of goals members of an organization should pursue and ideas about the appropriate kinds or standards of behavior organizational members should use to achieve these goals. From organizational values develop organizational norms, guidelines or expectations that prescribe appropriate kinds of behavior by employees in particular situations and control the behavior of organizational members towards one another.'

_____ is not the same as corporate culture.

a. Union shop
b. Organizational development
c. Organizational culture
d. Organizational effectiveness

9. _____ refers to increasing the spiritual, political, social or economic strength of individuals and communities. It often involves the empowered developing confidence in their own capacities.

The term Human _____ covers a vast landscape of meanings, interpretations, definitions and disciplines ranging from psychology and philosophy to the highly commercialized Self-Help industry and Motivational sciences.

a. Empowerment
b. A Stake in the Outcome
c. AAAI
d. A4e

10. _____ refers to the stock of skills and knowledge embodied in the ability to perform labor so as to produce economic value. It is the skills and knowledge gained by a worker through education and experience. Many early economic theories refer to it simply as labor, one of three factors of production, and consider it to be a fungible resource -- homogeneous and easily interchangeable.
a. Productivity management
b. Market structure
c. Deflation
d. Human capital

Chapter 17. Communication

1. _____ is a subfield of the larger discipline of communication studies. _____, as a field, is the consideration, analysis, and criticism of the role of communication in organizational contexts.

The field traces its lineage through business information, business communication, and early mass communication studies published in the 1930s through the 1950s.

   a. A4e
   b. AAAI
   c. A Stake in the Outcome
   d. Organizational communication

2. In attribution theory, the _____ is a theory describing cognitive tendency to predominantly over-value dispositional explanations for the observed behaviors of others, thus under-valuing or acknowledging the potentiality of situational attributions or situational explanations for the behavioral motives of others. In other words, people predominantly presume that the actions of others are indicative of the 'kind' of person they are, rather than the kind of situations that compels their behavior. However, the over attribution effect generally does not account for our own ability to self-justify our behaviors; we tend to prefer interpreting our own actions in terms of the situational variables accessible to our awareness.
   a. Pygmalion effect
   b. Confirmation bias
   c. Halo effect
   d. Fundamental attribution error

3. A _____ occurs when people attribute their successes to internal or personal factors but attribute their failures to situational factors beyond their control. The _____ can be seen in the common human tendency to take credit for success but to deny responsibility for failure. It may also manifest itself as a tendency for people to evaluate ambiguous information in a way that is beneficial to their interests.
   a. Halo effect
   b. Pygmalion effect
   c. Fundamental attribution error
   d. Self-serving bias

4. The _____(term coined by Herman Ebbinghaus), refers to the finding that recall accuracy varies as a function of an item's position within a study list. When asked to recall a list of items in any order (free recall), people tend to begin recall with the end of the list, recalling those items best (the recency effect.) Among earlier list items, the first few items are recalled more frequently than the middle items (the primacy effect.)
   a. 28-hour day
   b. Serial position effect
   c. 33 Strategies of War
   d. 1990 Clean Air Act

5. _____ is a term used in various branches of engineering and economic development.

_____ refers to small premises provided, often by local authorities or economic development agencies, to help new businesses to establish themselves. These typically provide not only physical space and utilities, but also administrative services and links to support and finance organisations, as well as peer support among the tenants.

a. Workspace
b. 33 Strategies of War
c. 1990 Clean Air Act
d. 28-hour day

Chapter 18. Managing Innovation and Change

1. A _____ or disruptive innovation is an innovation that improves a product or service in ways that the market does not expect, typically by being lower priced or designed for a different set of consumers.

Disruptive innovations can be broadly classified into low-end and new-market disruptive innovations. A new-market disruptive innovation is often aimed at non-consumption (i.e., consumers who would not have used the products already on the market), whereas a lower-end disruptive innovation is aimed at mainstream customers for whom price is more important than quality.

   a. Marketing strategy
   b. Green marketing
   c. Business-to-business
   d. Disruptive technology

2. A _____ is a framework for creating economic, social, and/or other forms of value. The term _____ is thus used for a broad range of informal and formal descriptions to represent core aspects of a business, including purpose, offerings, strategies, infrastructure, organizational structures, trading practices, and operational processes and policies.

Conceptualizations of _____s try to formalize informal descriptions into building blocks and their relationships.

   a. Gap analysis
   b. Business networking
   c. Business model
   d. Business model design

3. _____ of the learning curve effect and the closely related experience curve effect express the relationship between equations for experience and efficiency or between efficiency gains and investment in the effort. The experience of 'learning curves' was first observed by the 19th Century German psychologist Hermann Ebbinghaus according to the difficulty of memorizing varying numbers of verbal stimuli, and subsequent learning about the complex processes of learning are discussed in the

The rule used for representing the learning curve effect states that the more times a task has been performed, the less time will be required on each subsequent iteration.

   a. Spatial Decision Support Systems
   b. Distribution
   c. Point biserial correlation coefficient
   d. Models

4. _____ is a theory in evolutionary biology which states that most sexually reproducing species will experience little evolutionary change for most of their geological history (in an extended state called stasis.) When evolution occurs, it is localized in rare, rapid events of branching speciation (called cladogenesis.) Cladogenesis is simply the process by which species split into two distinct species, rather than one species gradually transforming into another.

   a. 33 Strategies of War
   b. 1990 Clean Air Act
   c. Punctuated equilibrium
   d. 28-hour day

5. _____ is an idea in the field of Organizational studies and management which describes the psychology, attitudes, experiences, beliefs and Values (personal and cultural values) of an organization. It has been defined as 'the specific collection of values and norms that are shared by people and groups in an organization and that control the way they interact with each other and with stakeholders outside the organization.'

   This definition continues to explain organizational values also known as 'beliefs and ideas about what kinds of goals members of an organization should pursue and ideas about the appropriate kinds or standards of behavior organizational members should use to achieve these goals. From organizational values develop organizational norms, guidelines or expectations that prescribe appropriate kinds of behavior by employees in particular situations and control the behavior of organizational members towards one another.'

   _____ is not the same as corporate culture.

   a. Organizational development
   b. Union shop
   c. Organizational effectiveness
   d. Organizational culture

6. _____ is a structured approach to transitioning individuals, teams, and organizations from a current state to a desired future state. The current definition of _____ includes both organizational _____ processes and individual _____ models, which together are used to manage the people side of change.

   A number of models are available for understanding the transitioning of individuals through the phases of _____ and strengthening organizational development initiative in both government and corporate sectors.

   a. Change Management
   b. 1990 Clean Air Act
   c. 28-hour day
   d. 33 Strategies of War

Chapter 18. Managing Innovation and Change

7. _____ has been described as the 'process of social influence in which one person can enlist the aid and support of others in the accomplishment of a common task'. A definition more inclusive of followers comes from Alan Keith of Genentech who said '_____ is ultimately about creating a way for people to contribute to making something extraordinary happen.'

_____ is one of the most salient aspects of the organizational context. However, defining _____ has been challenging.

 a. Situational leadership
 b. Leadership
 c. 28-hour day
 d. 1990 Clean Air Act

8. _____ of individual behavior or MARS BAR model of individual behavior or simply _____ is a model that seeks to explain individual behavior as a result of internal and external factors or influences acting together. The name of the model is an acronym for individual Motivation, Abilities, Role Perception and Situational Factors. These are seen as the four major factors in determining individual behavior and results.
 a. Teasing
 b. 28-hour day
 c. MARS model
 d. 1990 Clean Air Act

9. _____ refers to the movement of cash into or out of a business or financial product. It is usually measured during a specified, finite period of time. Measurement of _____ can be used

- to determine a project's rate of return or value. The time of _____s into and out of projects are used as inputs in financial models such as internal rate of return, and net present value.
- to determine problems with a business's liquidity. Being profitable does not necessarily mean being liquid. A company can fail because of a shortage of cash, even while profitable.
- as an alternate measure of a business's profits when it is believed that accrual accounting concepts do not represent economic realities. For example, a company may be notionally profitable but generating little operational cash (as may be the case for a company that barters its products rather than selling for cash.) In such a case, the company may be deriving additional operating cash by issuing shares evaluating default risk, re-investment requirements, etc.

_____ is a generic term used differently depending on the context. It may be defined by users for their own purposes.

Chapter 18. Managing Innovation and Change

a. Gross profit margin
b. Gross profit
c. Sweat equity
d. Cash flow

10. _____ is the discipline of planning, organizing and managing resources to bring about the successful completion of specific project goals and objectives. It is often closely related to and sometimes conflated with Program management.

A project is a finite endeavor--having specific start and completion dates--undertaken to meet particular goals and objectives, usually to bring about beneficial change or added value.

a. Precedence diagram
b. Project engineer
c. Work package
d. Project management

11. In business and engineering, new _____ is the term used to describe the complete process of bringing a new product or service to market. There are two parallel paths involved in the NProduct development process: one involves the idea generation, product design, and detail engineering; the other involves market research and marketing analysis. Companies typically see new _____ as the first stage in generating and commercializing new products within the overall strategic process of product life cycle management used to maintain or grow their market share.

a. 1990 Clean Air Act
b. 28-hour day
c. Product development
d. 33 Strategies of War

12. A _____ is a professional in the field of project management. _____s can have the responsibility of the planning, execution, and closing of any project, typically relating to construction industry, architecture, computer networking, telecommunications or software development.

Many other fields in the production, design and service industries also have _____s.

a. Work package
b. Project management
c. Project manager
d. Project engineer

Chapter 18. Managing Innovation and Change

13. A _____ is something for which there is demand, but which is supplied without qualitative differentiation across a market. It is a product that is the same no matter who produces it, such as petroleum, notebook paper, or milk. In other words, copper is copper.
    a. 28-hour day
    b. Commodity
    c. 33 Strategies of War
    d. 1990 Clean Air Act

14. _____, a business term, is a measure of how products and services supplied by a company meet or surpass customer expectation. It is seen as a key performance indicator within business and is part of the four perspectives of a Balanced Scorecard.

    In a competitive marketplace where businesses compete for customers, _____ is seen as a key differentiator and increasingly has become a key element of business strategy.

    a. Foreign ownership
    b. Horizontal integration
    c. Critical Success Factor
    d. Customer satisfaction

15. _____ describes how content an individual is with his or her job.

    The happier people are within their job, the more satisfied they are said to be. _____ is not the same as motivation, although it is clearly linked.

    a. Goal-setting theory
    b. Human relations
    c. Job analysis
    d. Job satisfaction

16. _____ is exchange of capital, goods, and services across international borders or territories. In most countries, it represents a significant share of gross domestic product (GDP.) While _____ has been present throughout much of history, its economic, social, and political importance has been on the rise in recent centuries.
    a. A Stake in the Outcome
    b. A4e
    c. AAAI
    d. International trade

Chapter 18. Managing Innovation and Change

17. In sociology and social psychology, _____ is the process through which people try to control the impressions other people form of them. It is a goal-directed conscious or unconscious attempt to influence the perceptions of other people about a person, object or event by regulating and controlling information in social interaction. It is usually used synonymously with self-presentation, if a person tries to influence the perception of their image.

   a. A Stake in the Outcome
   b. A4e
   c. AAAI
   d. Impression management

18. A _____ or transnational corporation is a corporation or enterprise that manages production or delivers services in more than one country. It can also be referred to as an international corporation.

The first modern _____ is generally thought to be the Dutch East India Company, established in 1602.

   a. Financial Accounting Standards Board
   b. Multinational corporation
   c. Small and medium enterprises
   d. Command center

19. _____ is a strategic planning method used to evaluate the Strengths, Weaknesses, Opportunities, and Threats involved in a project or in a business venture. It involves specifying the objective of the business venture or project and identifying the internal and external factors that are favorable and unfavorable to achieving that objective. The technique is credited to Albert Humphrey, who led a convention at Stanford University in the 1960s and 1970s using data from Fortune 500 companies.

   a. SWOT analysis
   b. Corporate image
   c. Marketing
   d. Market share

20. The _____ is a concept from business management that was first described and popularized by Michael Porter in his 1985 best-seller, Competitive Advantage: Creating and Sustaining Superior Performance.

A _____ is a chain of activities. Products pass through all activities of the chain in order and at each activity the product gains some value. The chain of activities gives the products more added value than the sum of added values of all activities. It is important not to mix the concept of the _____ with the costs occurring throughout the activities.

a. Market development
b. Mass marketing
c. Customer relationship management
d. Value chain

ANSWER KEY

Chapter 1
1. d 2. b 3. d 4. d 5. b 6. d 7. c 8. b 9. b 10. a
11. a 12. b 13. d 14. a 15. d

Chapter 2
1. d 2. a 3. d 4. d 5. a 6. d 7. d 8. a 9. c 10. d
11. d 12. d 13. c 14. d 15. d 16. b 17. d 18. a 19. c 20. d
21. d 22. a 23. d 24. d 25. d 26. c 27. a 28. a

Chapter 3
1. b 2. d 3. d 4. d 5. d 6. d 7. b 8. a 9. d 10. d
11. d 12. d 13. b 14. c 15. c 16. d 17. c 18. d 19. c 20. c
21. d 22. d 23. d 24. d 25. d

Chapter 4
1. d 2. b 3. d 4. c 5. a 6. d 7. d 8. d

Chapter 5
1. b 2. c 3. d 4. d 5. d 6. c 7. d 8. a 9. d 10. b
11. d 12. d 13. d 14. a 15. c 16. c 17. d

Chapter 6
1. d 2. a 3. d 4. d 5. d 6. b 7. d 8. d 9. a 10. c
11. c 12. d 13. d 14. a 15. d 16. a 17. d 18. d 19. a 20. d

Chapter 7
1. a 2. b 3. d 4. d 5. b 6. d 7. b 8. b 9. b 10. c
11. d 12. d 13. c 14. d 15. c 16. d 17. d 18. d 19. d 20. c
21. c 22. d 23. b 24. c 25. d 26. d 27. d 28. a

Chapter 8
1. c 2. d 3. d 4. d 5. b 6. d 7. d 8. b 9. b

Chapter 9
1. b 2. c 3. d 4. c 5. d 6. d

Chapter 10
1. b 2. d 3. c 4. d 5. d 6. c 7. d 8. b 9. c

Chapter 11
1. d 2. a 3. a 4. d 5. d 6. b 7. b 8. d 9. b

Chapter 12
1. d	2. d	3. d	4. b	5. b	6. d	7. a	8. d	9. c	10. b
11. d	12. b	13. d	14. d	15. a	16. a	17. c	18. d	19. d	20. c
21. a	22. b	23. d	24. d	25. d	26. d	27. a	28. d	29. b	30. d
31. c									

Chapter 13
1. c	2. d	3. d	4. a	5. d	6. d	7. c	8. d	9. d	10. b
11. b	12. d	13. d	14. c	15. b	16. c	17. d	18. d	19. b	20. c
21. d	22. d	23. d							

Chapter 14
1. d	2. d	3. d	4. d	5. b	6. a	7. d	8. b	9. d	10. b
11. a	12. b	13. b	14. a	15. c					

Chapter 15
1. b	2. d	3. d	4. b	5. d	6. a	7. d	8. d	9. c

Chapter 16
1. d	2. d	3. b	4. c	5. d	6. c	7. c	8. c	9. a	10. d

Chapter 17
1. d	2. d	3. d	4. b	5. a

Chapter 18
1. d	2. c	3. d	4. c	5. d	6. a	7. b	8. c	9. d	10. d
11. c	12. c	13. b	14. d	15. d	16. d	17. d	18. b	19. a	20. d

www.ingramcontent.com/pod-product-compliance
Lightning Source LLC
Chambersburg PA
CBHW081846230426
43669CB00018B/2840